THEATRE LIBRARY ASSOCIATION

The Theatre Library Association is a non-profit organization established in 1937 to advance the interests of all those involved in collecting and preserving theatrical materials, and in utilizing those materials for purposes of scholarship. The membership is international and includes public and private institutions as well as librarians, cutarors, private collectors, historians, professors, theatre designers, actors, writers and all other interested persons.

The Theatre Library Association meets annually to conduct its business in the fall of each year. It presents a day of conferences and programs during the annual meeting of the American Library Association, usually in late spring or early summer.

Its publications are Broadside, *a quarterly newsletter, and* Performing Arts Resources, *an annual journal.*

It is governed by a constitution, which provides for a board of directors elected by the membership, and officers elected by the board.

THE THEATRE LIBRARY ASSOCIATION BOOK AWARDS

Two awards are presented annually for books of unusual merit and distinction in the fields served by the association.

The George Freedley Award, *established in 1968, honors a work in the field of theatre published in the United States. Only books with subjects related to live performance will be considered. They may be biography, history or criticism.*

The Theatre Library Association Award, *established in 1973, honors a book published in the United States in the field of recorded performance, which includes motion pictures, radio and television.*

Works ineligible for both awards are textbooks; anthologies; collections of essays previously published in other sources; reprints; works on dance, ballet and opera; plays or scripts; and other works at the discretion of the jurors. Translations of significant works, other than play texts, will be considered. Entries will be judged on the basis of scholarship, readability, and general contribution of knowledge to the fields served by the associaton. No galley sheets or proofs will be accepted. Books nominated for the awards must be published in the calendar year prior to the presentation of the awards and must be received no later than March 15 of the year following publication.

Nominations are to be submitted in writing to the Chairman of the Book Awards Committee, in care of the Theatre Library Association, 111 Amsterdam Avenue, New York, N.Y. 10023.

The 1976 George Freedley Award was presented to Jacques Callot: Artist of the Theatre *by Gerald Kahan* (University of Georgia Press). *Honorable Mention was awarded* Shakespeare on the American Stage *by Charles H. Shattuck* (Folger Shakespeare Library Press).

The 1976 Theatre Library Association Award was presented to The Good Guys, the Bad Guys and the First Amendment: Free Speech and Fairness in Broadcasting *by Fred W. Friendly* (Random House).

The logo for Performing Arts Resources *is a reduction of a design by Aubrey Beardsley for the cover of* Pierrot, *one of a series of books by Henry de Vere Stacpoole published in the late 1890s. I am indebted to my friend Marian Spitzer Thompson for suggesting it to me during my search for an appropriate visual identification for the publication of the Theatre Library Association.*   The Editor

PERFORMING ARTS RESOURCES

edited by Mary C. Henderson
with the assistance of Wendy Warnken

VOLUME FOUR

Published by the Theatre Library Association

The Library of Congress cataloged this serial as follows:

Performing Arts Resources
    Vols. for 1974- issued by the Theatre Library Association
    ISSN 0360-3814
1. Performing arts—Library resources—United States—
Periodicals. 1. Theatre Library Association
Z6935.P46   016.7902'08   75-646287
ISBN 0-932610-00-5

Produced by Publishing Center for Cultural Resources, NYC
Printed in the United States of America

TABLE OF CONTENTS

A MESSAGE FROM THE PRESIDENT OF THE
THEATRE LIBRARY ASSOCIATION

It is with great pleasure that I take this opportunity to welcome a new editor and to thank her predecessor for his work in beginning *Performing Arts Resources,* Theatre Library Association's annual volume devoted to research resources. With this edition of *PAR,* editorial work has been taken over by Mary C. Henderson, Curator of the Theatre and Music Collection, Museum of the City of New York, and a distinguished historian of the American theatre. She replaces Ted Perry, Curator of Film at the Museum of Modern Art, who has served TLA as founding editor and helped, through three editions of PAR, to establish it as a vital reference tool for librarians and historians of theatre, film, broadcasting, and, indeed, the whole field of performing arts.

I look forward to Mary Henderson's editorship, and urge members of TLA to aid her in every way possible with suggestions and contributions.

Brooks McNamara, President
Theatre Library Association

PERFORMING ARTS RESOURCES, *the annual publication of the Theatre Library Association, is designed to gather and disseminate scholarly articles dealing with (a) the location of resource materials relating to the theatre, film, television and radio and (b) a description, listing or evaluation of the contents of such collections, whether public or private.*

PAR *will not accept for publication critical or historical studies or general bibliographies of materials on deposit in more than one collection. Articles dealing with the dance and music are also excluded.*

All manuscripts must be submitted cleanly typed, one side only, double-spaced and adhering to the style and method described in the MLA Style Sheet, Second Edition. Since PAR *will attempt to cover a wide area, articles of extraordinary length or technical prolixity will be admissible only in rare circumstances. Photographs and illustrations may be used at the discretion of the editorial board.*

Please submit manuscripts with covering letter and return postage to:

> *Dr. Mary C. Henderson*
> *Theatre Collection*
> *Museum of the City of New York*
> *Fifth Avenue at 103rd Street*
> *New York, New York 10029*

AN EDITORIAL VIEW

In the closing moments of the 1976 SIBMAS conference in Vienna, one of the participants compared the week-long polyglot proceedings to a popular Viennese coffee concoction called *Melange*. Always listed at the bottom of the beverage list because of its high price, it consists of layers of rich and varied ingredients topped with the inevitable *Schlag*. It was indeed an apt simile. The meetings were certainly varied, sometimes heavy with content, occasionally laced with spice, and finally concluded with airy good will.

I have taken my inspiration from the conference and from its spirit of *Melange* in the preparation of this volume. It is devoted entirely to information about collections outside of the United States and to the methods, opinions, and aspirations of fellow curators, librarians, archivists, and professionals in the field. Some of the essays give comfort because they prove that we in America are not alone in our struggles and problems. Others reveal that our concerns are shared and our work is directed toward the same goals. While we may feel an occasional sting of envy when we read of the program in the Netherlands to preserve the essence of live production on film that is enthusiastically supported by the government and unions, we can take heart that we are making real strides in the preservation of our major performing arts collections.

Another inspiration for this volume came as an idea released by time. At the last ALA meeting held in New York some years ago, the Theatre Library Association invited Cornelia Otis Skinner to reflect aloud on her experiences in researching *Madame Sarah* in libraries abroad. We all had a merry time listening to her hilarious descriptions of the perils of overseas research and I wondered at the time how much was truth, how much was embroidery. On my own I have discovered that our breezy attitude toward libraries and collections best described as the where-is-the-photocopy-machine-and-how-much? school of research is lamentably and uniquely American. As Miss Skinner recalled, there is often a neat protocol that one must follow in order to use continental libraries and collections. In the case of the Russian collections, for instance, the scholar must conduct him or herself as if he or she were an officially appointed representative with notebook.

A final inspiration arose from the realization that Americans are scholarly gadflies. Financed by grants, floated on sabbatical leaves or driven to work/play holidays by the Internal Revenuers, they regularly take to the skies and eventually land on the steps of performing arts collections all over the world with the purpose of unearthing that still unpublished fact or bringing to light that undiscovered manuscript.

Although Andre Veinstein's *Performing Arts Collections: An International Handbook* remains (as it should) the traveling companion of everyone seeking information about collections across both oceans, this book attempts to provide a coda to a few of his citations and to introduce several new archives which have become established since the publication of his book.

New York, 1978   Mary C. Henderson

DAME NELLIE MELBA OR PEACH MELBA

by Peter Burgis

The English navigator Captain James (Jim) Cook is credited with discovering the great southern continent of Terra Australia in 1770. The initial settlement of 1788 was under the management of Governor Phillip, who directed a cast of pioneers chosen by the best judges in England. These bad good people were convicts of an artistic nature if judged by their offsprings' contribution to the world entertainment scene during the succeeding two hundred years.

The foundations of Australian show biz were laid during the middle 1800s coinciding with the discovery of gold. The local gold rush brought not only new settlers but a steady stream of entertainers from England, Europe and the Americas. The gold has long since petered out but the entertainers continue to flock here in increasing numbers.

Geographically isolated Australians have always delighted in being entertained and the financial rewards of a successful Australian season must have been considerable to induce the cream of the world's performing artists to undertake a fourteen-week return boat trip for the privilege of advancing their career in the antipodes. The fact that many performers made numerous visits is indicative of the lucrative rewards which awaited a successful artist, despite the small under-four million population which existed to 1901 when the colonies joined together to form a nation.

Apart from the joys of the sea voyage, visitors had to contend with horse-drawn coaches, bad roads, a warm climate, and hazards of drought, flood, and bushfire, not to mention bushrangers, our own breed of highwaymen. Despite these adversities, the entertainers accepted the challenge of traversing this hot arid continent, the size of the continental United States, and the show went on, even if it were in a tent or open field.

Celebrities that worked the Aussie circuit in the very early days included the Sousa Band, Lola Montez, the Besses O' The Barn

Peter Burgis is Sound Archivist of the National Library of Australia, Canberra.

Band, Sarah Bernhardt, Will Rogers, Grace Palotta, W.C. Fields, Lillian Nordica, Emma Calvé, Tom Thumb, the Sheffield Choir, and Harry Houdini. These pioneer visitors were followed by John McCormack, Dame Clara Butt, Feodor Chaliapin, Anna Pavlova, Richard Tauber, Sergei Rachmaninoff, Mischa Elman, Toti Dal Monte, Richard Crooks, Dame Sybil Thorndyke, Bob Hope, David Frost and literally thousands of others from all rungs of show business. Australia has also played host to hundreds of companies and groups of opera, drama, ballet, dance, vaudeville, choirs, orchestras, and minstrels as well as wild west shows and circuses.

We also applauded loudly the triumphant returns of sons and daughters who had ventured overseas to further their careers, such as Billy Williams, ex-Melbourne horse jockey, who journeyed to England in 1899, returning home in 1910 as a legend in the world of Music Hall and a creative giant in the art of making both disc and cylinder sound recordings.

Billy was not the first local artist to contribute to establishing a proper balance of trade in international performing artist exchanges. Back in 1847, a colonial lass, Eliza Winstanely, had wowed them at the Theatre Royal, Manchester, England. In the 1870s, a fellow countrywoman, Lucy Chambers, was praised in the United Kingdom for her singing. The 1880s saw the escalation of Australian performing artists seeking world stardom and the arrival on the European opera scene of Mrs. Helen Armstrong stunned the operatic world as she established herself rapidly as the greatest soprano voice of her time. Using a surname corruption of her birthplace, Melbourne, she became the first Australian person to become an international household name. Madame Nellie Melba was Australia to the world long before any politician or sportsman, or even kangaroo.

Others who carved out international careers include operatic and concert artists Frances Alda, Ada Crossley, Peter Dawson, Dame Joan Hammond, Marjorie Lawrence, Joan Sutherland and June Bronhill; actors Leo McKern, Keith Mitchell, Cyril Ritchard, Oscar Asche, Marie Lohr, Dame Judith Anderson, Diane Cilento and Zoe Caldwell; and movie stars Errol Flynn, Merle Oberon, Peter Finch, Alec Kellaway and Rod Taylor. Dance and music are represented by Sir Robert Helpmann, Freddie Carpenter, Kenneth Rowell, Jan Rydenyi, Percy Grainger, Eileen Joyce, William Murdoch, Geoffrey Parsons,

Richard Bonynge, George Thalben-Ball, Sir William McKie, Ernest Hutcheson, Arthur Benjamin, Charles Mackerras, and Alex Lithgow. Popular entertainment has been enriched by the talents of Florrie Forde, Billy Williams, the Bee Gees, the Seekers, Frank Ifield, Lana Cantrell, Olivia Newton-John, Helen Reddy, Albert Whelan, Graeme Bell, May Worth, Annette Kellerman, Jean Hugard and Con Colleano.

The nation has also fostered film, television, and recorded sound industries which have been responsible for feeding many thousands of performing artists since their inception. The earliest showing of optical illusions and movement in this country dates back to 1896. In 1900, the Salvation Army produced an audiovisual presentation entitled *Soldiers Of The Cross*, described as a true concept of the biblical epic, combining moving film, slides, music and lecture. *Soldiers Of The Cross* ran for two hours and fifteen minutes.

In 1906, Australian filmmakers produced the world's first full-length feature film, *The Story Of The Kelly Gang*. This production was 4000 feet long and ran for sixty-five minutes, as compared to the 1903 American one-reeler, *The Great Train Robbery*, which was a mere 800 feet and lasted twenty minutes.

Up to the advent of sound motion pictures, Australian film men had produced some 300 full length feature films, an estimated 4000 newsreels and thousands of documentaries. Since 1930 when the talkies arrived, 300 feature films have been completed, together with many thousands of newsreels, documentaries and advertising films. The Film Archive of the National Library of Australia has preserved about ten percent of the pre-1930 silent productions and while it is unlikely that many more films from this period will be uncovered, a continual search and rescue operation is conducted by the small staff engaged on this project. The majority of the post-1930 films made in this country do still exist, with many in private collections. Fortunately, the bulk of films made in this period is held in the National Library collection, which also includes advertising materials, billboard posters, stills and other film memorabilia.

The National Library Film Archive has made rapid and worthwhile progress in recent years but unfortunately the action appears too late to rectify the tragic tale of document destruction that has characterized the first forty years of the local industry. The opportunity to preserve the recollections and personal papers of the early writers, directors, producers and cameramen was never fully grasped and has resulted in incomplete histories. The pioneers who have lived into the present are well represented, but others remain simply names in the history books.

Color television came to Australia in 1975 following nineteen years of black and white programs. The National Library Film Archive has managed to gather together a respectable cross-section of black and white programs, which represent material from the Government financed Australian Broadcasting Commission, as well as from the fifty or so commercial stations which service the nation. Although production of local television drama, quiz shows, and musicals has been abundant, increasing emphasis has been apparent in recent years in production of television documentaries and public affairs/news programs. Producing companies have agreed to co-operate with the National Library which will systematically acquire and preserve representative samples of all worthwhile future television programs. It is unfortunate that the inaugural 1956-60 period will remain poorly represented in the Library collection since it appears that little transmission from this period still exists.

In 1924, Australia had four radio stations operating with an estimated listening audience of about 3000 people. Ten years later, almost 100 stations were using the air waves to provide listening facilities to an audience of one million. Today, more than 300 stations operate with an audience difficult to estimate but involving most of the community at some stage each week.

From about 1933, the Australian radio industry commenced producing regular series of drama, comedy, music and quiz shows which became an every day part of life for most citizens. Tens of thousands of productions flourished during the next twenty-three years until the advent of television in 1956.

Local programs were often modelled on such American series as *Tarzan* (with Rod Taylor) or *Superman*, while home grown products like *Dad and Dave of Snake Gully* and *The Search for the Golden Boomerang* also proved very popular. Many of these serials operated for five, ten, or fifteen years, and were heard five times a week. The radio industry did nothing in this country to preserve its own history and when the National Collection of Sound Recordings was established by the National Library in 1973, it found that transcription discs of all types were strewn across the country in private collections and on rubbish heaps.

While it is unlikely at this late stage that a complete representation of all original Australian radio programs can be created, it is heartening to report that more than 60,000 discs have been found and directed to the National Library archive. Arrangements have also been reached with some major program producers for material of historic interest, both retrospective and current, to be donated to the Library collection. Despite these developments it is sad to reflect that less than one percent of all current creative and worthwhile broadcasting is being gathered by the National Library. This situation reflects shortages and financial restraints, which I trust that future generations will understand as they evaluate our wisdom, foresight and national awareness.

The commercial development of talking machines in this country occurred in the 1890s. From the very beginning of the industry, we were fortunate to enjoy a hybrid existence whereby we had available recordings from England, Europe and the Americas, both in disc and cylinder. Early Australian recording artists established their careers overseas because with the exception of two short-lived cylinder companies, the local recording of artists was not possible until the mid-1920s when World Record and Columbia set up recording studios. At this same time, Australian companies like H.M.V. and Brunswick were pressing overseas masters.

Until the depression, the local record manufacturing industry boomed and sales figures of from thirty to forty thousand for a 78 rpm record were not uncommon. The depression sent all the small companies into bankruptcy and forced the amalgamation of the "Big Three," H.M.V., Columbia and Parlophone, which formed the nucleus of what we now know as E.M.I. From the mid-1930s until the end of World War II, E.M.I. issued the bulk of its English and American catalogue in Australia. The 1942 E.M.I. Catalogue was over 600 pages thick and listed more than 30,000 titles which was considerable for a relatively small market. Following the end of World War II, remarkable growth in the recorded sound industry turned it into a commercial success which employs either directly or indirectly tens of thousands of people. It has reached the stage where the public buy more LP discs each year than they do books. The first LP discs appeared on the Australian market in 1952 and in 1960, the arrival of local stereo recording coincided with the production of the last 78 rpm disc. During the period 1925-60, approximately 10,000 titles were recorded in local studios, usually featuring Australian performers and often playing local compositions. Since 1960, the recording of local artists has continued to accelerate. Some Australian performers can now boast of having more than twenty LPs to their credit.

The only institution collecting sound recordings in a substantial way is the Music and Sound Recordings Section of the National Library whose holdings now exceed 260,000 discs, 5000 tapes, and 4000 cylinders. Despite the absence of deposit laws on new releases this compulsory collection embraces more than one million titles. Unfortunately, the bulk of the collection is not catalogued and is inaccessible. In fact, it is stored outside the main building in environmental conditions that would not be tolerated for sturdier printed materials. The only consolation is that future archivists will have a fine collection to put into order should it survive its current tribulations. It is a general pattern in Australian libraries that non-book material receive lowest priority and preference. Australia must look to its private collectors for instruction in the preservation of sound recordings and technology of reproducing vintage editions.

The staffs of libraries are trained in acquisition, cataloguing and retrieval. They are usually hampered in carrying out these duties by inadequate staffing, poor facilities, and lack of money. In Australia, the holdings by major libraries of performing arts documents is so meagre that the special problems created by such collections cannot be comfortably handled by the library staff which lacks the training and equipment with which to cope with them. This is coupled frequently with prejudice of the very physical nature of performing arts documents in a library environment. To be specific, very few library staffs can correctly handle an LP disc, nor are they familiar with the principles of reproduction and the operation of reproduction equipment. They are also unfamiliar with the sound recording trade and the processes of manufacture and distribution. Often they know little about the broad spectrum of recording artists, both current and retrospective, and in many cases are unable to differentiate between the abilities of LP, reel tape and audio cassette modes.

For archival preservation, it is necessary to also have experience in the host of technical developments associated with sound recording history, such as the difference between lateral cut and vertical cut discs, which is as elementary as the difference between a hardcover book and a paperback. It is essential to understand the technology of recording, reproducing and re-recording functions and techniques, as well as grasp the history of the recording companies and recording artists through biographical and discographical study and research. Library workers handling sound recordings should be as familiar with the names of Ben Selvin, Orrin Blackstone, and Eldridge Johnson as with James Joyce, Caxton, and *The Reader's Digest.*

Where attempts have been made in Australian institutions to develop performing arts collections, the supervision is often done by music librarians, who in addition to basic library skills of selection, acquisition, cataloguing and retrieval, are trained in music composition and playing a musical instrument. The music librarianship course ignores most forms of music apart from the classics and provides no study provision in the history of Australian performing artists and composers, especially in relation to film, video and sound recording documents. Graduates of this course are usually not interested in nor acquainted with popular culture, especially in areas of hillbilly, jazz and dance music, not to mention circus and vaudeville.

Australian library course curricula and librarianship educationists fail to grapple with the special problems of non-book materials. One can almost excuse the senior librarian with forty years experience for being unaware of these changes but there is no excuse for turning out graduates in the 1970s with no experience or instruction in the management of audiovisual library material. This situation is severely restricting the development of preserving arts archives as it limits the staff's ability to expand the collections. The staffing answer for preservation of performing arts documents seems to be the establishment of a hybrid team of historian, librarian and technical staff. Librarians do not necessarily make good archivists and performing arts historians and administrators are not that accomplished at cataloguing and retrieval. The training of librarian staff in audiovisual documents and technology is long overdue, and I am sure would be welcomed by such people.

National pride can only exist if we are proud of the good things from our past and are conscious of the necessity to preserve them for all to remember. History does not preserve itself. A determined and responsible program has to be instigated if the achievements of the entertainment industry in Australia are to be preserved and appreciated. There are a few bright spots on the horizon. The Governments of South Australia and Victoria are both examining the desirability of establishing two specialized performing arts collections at this time. The South Australian proposal involves the additional bonus of incorporating a collection illustrating the vintage technology that has entertained the nation, such as music boxes, horn gramophones, hand-wound projectors, magic lanterns, and similar mechanical wonders from the past. As projects of immense educational value there can be no argument. It is also obvious that such collections could be developed as tourist attractions of international stature. Both these proposals could succeed if they are created with some degree of autonomy that will encourage enterprise, receive adequate funding and are staffed with a well-balanced team of entertainment historians, librarians and technical staff, all capable of promoting the developments in a business-like manner.

Both Governments can be assured that the bulk of the performing arts history of Australia is still waiting to be gathered from many sources within the community for documentation and preservation as a monument to the achievements of the singers, musicians, composers and entertainers who helped establish and entertain this great nation. We have to decide whether we want our children to remember Dame Nellie Melba for what she did for this country, or whether she be remembered as the commercial basis of a fruit concoction.

RESEARCH OPPORTUNITIES AT THE THEATRE INSTITUTE LIBRARY, BARCELONA

by Joyce Duncan Falk

Just off the bustling Ramblas, in the exquisite Güell mansion designed by Catalonia's most famous architect, Antonio Gaudí, is one of the most important theatre collections in Europe and certainly the most extensive collection of Spanish drama outside the National Library in Madrid. In 1951 the Spanish poet and dramatist, Joaquín Montaner, claimed that all scholars and bibliophiles, specialists and amateurs of the Spanish drama were aware of the existence of the theatre collection of don Arturo Sedó in Barcelona but that few really knew the extent of the collection or its particular strengths. (1) More than twenty-five years later there is still too much truth to Montaner's assertion despite his own published selective catalogue and the public access to the collection provided by the Library and Museum of the Theatre Institute of Barcelona (Biblioteca y Museo del Instituto del Teatro, Diputación Provincial de Barcelona).

Sedó began his collection in earnest in 1941 with the purchase of the libraries and archives of theatrical publishers; he added, through Montaner's assistance, the collections of the scholars Emilio Cotarelo y Mori and José, Luis, and Aureliano Fernández Guerra. Other major acquisitions were the collections of the dramatist-journalist-scholar Narciso Díaz de Escovar of Málaga, and the Catalonian impresario, José Canals (Montaner, pp. 13-28). The private Sedó collection was open to scholars, but since its founder's death in the early 1960s, access had been severely limited. Catalonians in general and Spanish theatre scholars in particular are indeed fortunate that the Diputación Provincial was able to purchase the collection from Sedó's heirs

---

(1) Joaquín Montaner, *La Colección teatral de don Arturo Sedó* (Barcelona, 1951), p. 13. The collection is listed in André Veinstein, ed., *Performing Arts Libraries and Museums of the World*, 2d ed. (Paris, 1967), pp. 170-72.

Dr. Falk is the Director of the American Bibliographical Center in Santa Barbara, California.

and not only retain it in Barcelona but also provide convenient access to it.

The Theatre Institute, to which the Sedó collection now belongs, is the major center of theatre education in Catalonia. It was founded in 1913 as the Catalan School of Dramatic Art and is under the jurisdiction of the provincial government of Barcelona. (2) Its museum, the largest theatre museum in Spain, was founded in 1932 by Marc Jesús Bertran as the Museum of Scenic Art (Museo del Arte Escénico) and in 1954 was moved to the Palacio Güell at Conde del Asalto, 3. (3) The museum has its own archives, independent of the library. In addition to the permanent displays, the Institute mounts temporary exhibitions of a wide variety of theatrical activities of interest to both theatre aficionados and the general public. With the 1969 acquisition of the majority of the Sedó collection, more than 60,000 books and manuscripts plus an estimated million photographs, autographs, letters and theatre programs of the Sedó collection have now been made accessible to the public with the opening of the library. Although a number of items were placed in the Biblioteca de Cataluña, Barcelona, the Institute Library has become a major theatre research center as a result of the Sedó accessions.

In this small, intimate library the glass-enclosed bookcases of Sedó's original library complement the intriguing decor by Gaudí, who was as much a decorative artist as an architect. Bespectacled scholars peering over musty old manuscripts and crackling books sit alongside fresh students and intense theatre professionals. In 1973, the number of users averaged less than 200 per month; at present, the average is about 300 per month. They are a mixture of Institute students, professionals and aficionados of the theatre in Barcelona, and a few scholars from Spanish universities and foreign institutions. (4)

Current holdings are approximately 100,000 books and manu-

(2) Xavier Fàbregas, "Algunos aspectos de la investigación teatral," San Jorge, No. 81 (1971), p. 51.

(3) Museo del arte escénico del Instituto del Teatro: catálogo-guía (Barcelona: Diputacion Provincial de Barcelona, 1961).

(4) I am particularly grateful to Professor Xavier Fàbregas, Head of the Department of Research and Publications; Mr. Francisco Galmés, Administrator; and Miss Ana Vázquez, Librarian, for their warm interest and generosity in explaining the organization and operation of the library as well as in providing access to the collection.

scripts, of which about eighty percent are on Spanish theatre. This figure includes general reference books, play texts, and current theatre books as well as the retrospective research collection. The most valuable research materials, primarily from the Sedó collection, comprise four groups: (a) the Golden Age (sixteenth and seventeenth centuries) editions and manuscripts; (b) the *teatro menor* of the seventeenth and eighteenth centuries; (c) Catalan theatre of the nineteenth and twentieth centuries; and (d) the fugitive items such as theatre programs, documents and memorabilia.

The Golden Age materials are in both printed and manuscript form. Among the rare and valuable editions are a first edition, in perfect condition, of Cervante's *Ocho comedias y entremeses*, 1615; a complete and beautifully bound copy of the second edition of Juan de la Cueva's *Primera parte de las comedias y tragedias* (Seville, 1588), the first edition of which is not extant; and a 1525 Italian translation of Rojas's *Celestina*. The Lope de Vega editions include the *Comedias del famoso poeta* [*Parte I*] (Zaragoza, 1603); several seventeenth-century Barcelona and Zaragoza editions of the *Partes* of *Comedias*; a first edition of *La Dorotea* (1632); *La Vega del Parnaso* (Madrid, 1637); and the 1644 collection of autos sacramentales, loas, and entremeses, *Fiestas del Santíssimo Sacramento*. Similarly, dramatists like Moreto, Vélez de Guevara, Juan del Encina, Tirso de Molina, and Lope de Rueda are represented by examples of their early editions, some of which are very rare. There are important variant editions in the collection such as the seventeenth-century *La Vida es sueño* of Calderón, without place or date of publication; and Bartolomé de Torres Naharros's *La Propaladia* (Sevilla: Zingos, 1545). A relatively unknown edition of *La Victoria de Cristo* (Zaragoza, 1563) by Bartolemé de Palau is listed in Montaner's catalogue whereas the earliest edition previously known was that of Zaragoza, 1569. (5) Of the forty-eight volumes of the *Colección antigua de comedias de los mejores ingenios de España* (1652-1704), the Institute Library is lacking only seven volumes and parts of five more volumes; it is claimed that no library has a complete set. (6)

---

(5) Montaner, p. 55; José Simón Díaz, *Manual de bibliografía de la literatura española*, 2d ed. (Barcelona, 1966), p. 249.

(6) Dolores Givanel de Pujol, "La Colección teatral de don Arturo Sedó, vista por su bibliotecaria," *San Jorge*, No. 73 (1969), p. 26; Montaner, pp. 39-42.

The library is rich in manuscript copies and has a number of outstanding autograph manuscripts. Perhaps the most spectacular of these is Calderón's *El Agua mansa*, with his signature and the license of 1673. In addition there are autograph manuscripts by Lope de Vega (the entremes *El Hidalgo*), Belmonte y Bermúdez (*Amor desafiado* and others), Diamante (*La Cruz de Caravaca*, signed and dated 1664, and *El Mancebo de camino*), Vélez de Guevara (*La Cristianísima lis*), and Rojas Zorrilla and Vélez de Guevara (*El Catalán Serrallonga el bandolero*). There are also many eighteenth-century editions and adaptations of the Golden Age authors.

As valuable as the Golden Age materials are, it is in the *teatro menor* or *género chico* of the seventeenth and eighteenth centuries — the shorter theatrical pieces called entremeses, sainetes, loas, moji-gangas, jácaras, bailes, tonadillas, fines de fiesta, and unipersonales — that the Theatre Institute Library uniquely excels and offers the most opportunities for research today. These short dramatic pieces, often featuring singing and dancing, embellished all theatrical per-formances from the seventeenth through the early nineteenth cen-turies. The study of the *teatro menor* not only provides a great deal of data for social and literary history but also can yield considerable information on dramatic art and the theatre itself, as the short pieces often refer directly to the theatre.

The predominant type of *teatro menor* was the entremés until the middle of the eighteenth century when it was superseded by the sainete. Both the entremés and the sainete were short comic plays performed between the acts of a full-length play. The collection of entremeses in the Theatre Institute Library is by no means complete, but it is as large in number of titles as the collection of entremeses in the National Library in Madrid; both libraries have some items not found in the other. The Institute Library contains the oldest of the collections of entremeses by various authors, *Entremeses nuevos de diversos autores* (Zaragoza, 1640), which is, of course, a very impor-tant item in the teatro menor bibliography. The rarest of the hold-ings of this type is the unique copy of the *Ramillete gracioso* (Valen-cia, 1643), containing twenty-six entremeses rarely found in either early or modern editions. (7) Another very rare early collection is the two-part *Rasgos del ocio en diferentes bayles, entremeses, y loas de diversos autores* (Madrid, 1661 and 1664) with twenty-seven and

twenty-five pieces respectively. (8) Besides these most important collections, and several more not enumerated here, there are fragments
of other collections of interest to scholars such as the one of *Donaires
del gusto* (Madrid, 1642) found in the volume labeled "Entremeses.
Tomo desconocido. Fragmentos" and identified by Hannah Bergman (pp. 14-16). Holdings of single authors include the *Flor de
sainetes* by Francisco Navarrete y Ribera (Madrid, 1640), a very rare
work according to Montaner (p. 116) ; at least half a dozen original
manuscripts by Benavente and more than two dozen manuscript
copies of his entremeses and bailes; and manuscripts by Aguado,
Moreto, Monteser, and Moncín, among others. In short, there are
over forty volumes of collections of entremeses of the seventeenth and
eighteenth centuries, plus thirty volumes of individual printings
(*sueltas*), and five volumes of manuscripts (Bergman, p. 13).

This same type of short theatrical piece was designated by the
word "sainete," which, although occasionally used in the seventeenth
century, became the prevalent term from the 1760s into the first
quarter of the nineteenth century. The Theatre Institute Library
owns the two major collections—possibly the only collections—of
eighteenth-century sainetes published as collections: the two-volume,
eighty-sainete *Colección de saynetes representados en los teatros de
esta corte* (Madrid: Quiroga, 1791-1792) ; (9) and the forty-sainete
Colección escogida de saynetes modernos (Barcelona: Piferrer,
n.d.). (10) These copies, although not unique, are certainly rare.
Neither of them has been located in other libraries of Barcelona and

---

(7) Hannah E. Bergman, "Los Entremeses postcervantinos de la Biblioteca y Museo
del Instituto del Teatro de Barcelona," *Estudios Escénicos: Cuadernos de investigación teatral*, No. 14 [1971], p. 13. Contents are listed in Montaner, pp. 117-125.

(8) For an evaluation of its rarity and the list of contents of the second volume (1664),
see Montaner, pp. 142-150.

(9) This copy contains the proscribed sainete, *Los Payos hechizados*, which is missing
from the copy at the British Museum. At least two copies of this collection exist in the
United States (*National Union Catalog Pre-1956 Imprints*, 114, p. 669, lists the
Boston Public Library and the University of Minnesota copies).

(10) All but eight of the titles in the Barcelona-Piferrer collection have been established as eighteenth-century sainetes by virtue of the authors' dates, earlier printings,
or manuscripts. Piferrer's printings are generally considered late eighteenth-century,
but the collection could possibly have been printed early in the nineteenth century.
The collection does not appear in the British Museum, *General Catalogue of Printed
Books* (London, 1965), nor in the *N.U.C.*

Madrid. The contents of both collections were also published separately as *sueltas* so that there are numerous individual copies and examples in various factitious or binders' collections in the library. Collections of sainetes by a single author are more generally available in other libraries, but these, too, are fully represented here. For example, the library holds the earliest editions as well as the important later editions of the works of the two best-known authors of sainetes, Ramón de la Cruz and Juan Gonzalez del Castillo. In all, the number of sainetes in *suelta* editions in the library runs in the thousands and the number of manuscript copies in the hundreds.

Of the most important sainete author, Ramón de la Cruz, the library has several manuscripts in his own hand; over two dozen eighteenth-century manuscript copies. The latter are copies made for the eminent scholar of Spanish theatre, Emilio Cotarelo y Mori, from manuscripts now in the Biblioteca Municipal of Madrid (some of which were previously in the Archivo Municipal). Although at first appearance of little value, except as momentos of Cotarelo's voluminous work, they do enable the researcher at the Institute in Barcelona to compare various Cruz manuscripts and editions to the Madrid items, at least until photocopies or microfilms of the original manuscripts can be added to the Institute's collection.

The eighteenth-century manuscript copies of sainetes are frequently acting copies or copies submitted for licensing. The acting copies supply information about the actual performance of the work in terms of textual emendations, casts, stage business, and properties. The licensing copies show the kind of censorship applied by both civil and ecclesiastical authorities by deletion of material from the piece and by the written comments of the censors.

Much of this *teatro menor* is not available in modern editions, (11) nor is it available in any great quantity in libraries outside Madrid and Barcelona; therefore, the existence of such a large number of collections, fragments of collections, *suelta* editions, and manuscripts

---

(11) Some examples, however, are Felicidad Buendía, ed., *Antologia del entremes (desde Lope de Rueda hasta Antonio de Zamora): Siglos XVI y XVII* (Madrid, 1965; Hannah E. Bergman, ed., *Ramillete de entremeses y bailes..., Siglo XVII* (Madrid, 1970); and the older, pioneering collection by Emilio Cotarelo y Mori, *Colección de entremeses, loas, bailes, jácaras y mojigangas desde fines del siglo XVI a mediados del XVIII*, Nueva Biblioteca de Autores Españoles, 17 and 18 (Madrid, 1911).

in one place greatly facilitates the investigation not only of literary and bibliographical questions, but also the numerous aspects of theatre history, especially the diffusion of popular theatrical activity throughout Spain during the seventeenth and eighteenth centuries.

The third major area of emphasis in the collection of the Theatre Institute Library is quite naturally Catalan theatre, which is, for the most part, a nineteenth- and twentieth-century phenomenon. The materials of this period in the library are by no means limited to Catalan authors, as a glance at Montaner's selected catalogue quickly shows, but it is in Catalan theatre that the library is particularly rich and can be expected to continue to acquire current and retrospective materials. The holdings consist of theatre archives, printed texts, autograph manuscripts, and manuscript copies of both full-length plays and the *teatro menor* forms. Among the more interesting items are the illustrated bilingual sainetes (Catalan-Spanish), the manuscripts of non-published works by lesser Catalan dramatists, and the autograph manuscript of the poet Jacinto Verdaguer's only dramatic work, *L'adoració dels pastors*. The better-known authors such as Federico Soler ("Pitarra"), José María de Sagarra, Santiago Rusiñol, and Angel Guimerá are represented by a great number of autographed manuscripts. Although there has been no consistent collection of the archives of Barcelona theatres, much less of theatres of the province, some have been acquired, most notably those of the Romea theatre from 1865 to 1930, and the Novedades and Tívoli theatres, which were all under the direction of the impresario José Canals. A portion of these archives is being published in the Institute's journal beginning with "Estrenos en al Teatro Romea de Barcelona: 1. Septiembre-diciembre de 1865," *Estudios Escénicos*, No. 15 (July 1972), pp. 41-50. In early 1973, the collection of the scholar Frencesc Curat was acquired, which added correspondence, press clippings, and other items pertinent to early twentieth-century Catalan theatre. Now that there is an operating library to care for their records, it would be logical for current Barcelona theatres to be more interested in providing at least a complete set of programs and posters of each season, and to realize the value of the library's functioning as a depository for their archives. Then the Institute Library could truly serve as an information center for scholars of contemporary Catalan theatre.

The resources of the Theatre Institute Library go beyond books and manuscripts to include a wide variety of fugitive materials and documents, mostly from the Sedó collection, spanning the period from the second quarter of the nineteenth century to the mid-twentieth century. Among the theatre programs, records, contracts, sketches, scene designs, scores, and librettos, are the programs of the Teatro Real of Madrid, mid-nineteenth century to 1925, many with notes and comments by the Infanta Isabel de Borbón; programs of the Teatro del Balón of Cadiz, 1859-1862; programs of the Teatro de la Cruz, Madrid, 1831-1833; and a list of theatrical companies of 1866-1867 and a statement of accounts for 1880-1881 from the Teatro Principal of Valencia. There are programs (1827-1828, 1831-1833, and 1835), daily expense accounts, subscription receipts and a statement of accounts of 1827 from the Teatro del Príncipe, Madrid; and a printed list of the sainetes performed in the Cruz and Príncipe theatres, 1823-1829.

Another type of material is a small number of documents concerning the regulation of theatrical activity: municipal orders, prohibitions and *bandos* in Barcelona, Madrid, and Málaga. These are scattered from the seventeenth to the nineteenth century and do not constitute an important collection, but would be of interest to anyone studying such regulations.

The remainder of the materials consist of photographs of theatrical personalities, authors and productions; press clippings; miscellaneous programs; sketches; scores and librettos; letters; and simply autographs. Sedó has been called a fanatic of the theatrical world, collecting everything from the rarest manuscript to the casual photograph or autograph of a passing performer. All of these materials are carefully indexed in their respective sections of the card catalogue. In addition, the library is currently in the process of indexing the Archivo Tomás, a collection of press clippings and articles on theatre from periodicals of various countries during the years 1920-1930. Of the total of 6000 items, those of most significance, the 2400 Spanish ones, have already been indexed.

Access to the entire collection at the Theatre Institute Library is provided through a series of catalogues. The main catalogue for books and manuscripts is a title catalogue, originally of the Sedó collection and now incorporating new titles as space permits. There are also an author catalogue, *documentos* catalogue (i.e., all the fugitive material, memorabilia, and documents), a subject index of recent acquisitions, and a title catalogue of newly received works awaiting incorporation into the main title catalogue. The library is open mornings and afternoons, Monday through Friday; on Saturdays and during the summer months it is open only in the mornings. There are excellent copying facilities on the premises and arrangements may be made for microfilming. For more general books and reference resources and some additional works on Spanish theatre, the researcher has to walk only a few blocks to the main public library of the province, the Biblioteca de Cataluña, one of the most progressive of Spanish libraries.

The conjunction of the Theatre Institute Library and the Biblioteca de Cataluña invites further investigations by theatre and library scholars. Materials exist for literary and bibliographical studies, and for studies of Spanish printing, publishing, graphic arts used in illustrations of theatrical pieces, theatrical companies, musical theatre and dance (opera, zarzuela, tonadilla), and for the investigation of aspects of social history, especially the entertainment of the masses who have often been excluded from traditional history.

HISTORY IN MOTION

by Geoffrey Wigoder

To reconstruct the early periods of mankind, the historian is thrown back to meager archeological remains. From these clues he builds up his picture of major developments as well as of everyday life. A revolution came with the availability of written records, and as these became more plentiful and accessible, so the task of re-creating and interpreting the past became more profound and rich. A further revolution has occurred over the past century with the invention of the means to record permanently through film and sound the great events as well as the everyday life of man and people. The historical significance and usages of film are now being realized and exploited. Country after country is establishing a national film archive, so as to preserve films of historic importance. But so far there has been no such film archive in a Jewish context.

Literally thousands of films have been made on topics of Jewish interest in the course of this century, when, it has been said, the Jewish people has had more history than any other people. Such climactic events as the destruction of European Jewry by the Nazis, the development of Jewish settlement in Israel and the establishment and activities of the Jewish state, the growth of American Jewry and its emergence to a position of leadership on the world Jewish scene have been faithfully recorded from many viewpoints in films. But hitherto these films have been scattered in many hands in various countries. No systematic attempt has been made to preserve them. Moreover, no effort has been made to save the extensive documentation that exists. As a result a vast quantity of invaluable and irreplaceable material that shows the actual face of Jewish history has already been destroyed and lost.

The gap is now being filled by the Abraham F. Rad Contemporary Jewish Film Archives, established in 1972 under the joint auspices of the Hebrew University and the World Zionist Organiza-

Dr. Wigoder is Director of the Abraham F. Rad Contemporary Jewish Film Archive.

tion on the Mount Scopus Campus of the University, with the object of locating, listing and collecting films of Jewish content and interest from all parts of the world. The archive has been made possible through the generosity of the Iranian philanthropist Abraham F. Rad, for whom it is named.

The Rad Archives is linked with the Jewish National and University Library, the world repository for all Jewish documentation, and represents an extra dimension to scholars of Jewish history in this century. It is administered by the Hebrew University's Institute of Contemporary Jewry which is playing a central role in interpreting world Jewry to Israelis and Israel to world Jewry.

The successful development of this Archive presents the challenge of gathering and preserving the actual sound and sight of Jewish history and the Jewish world. The rapid speed of events adds a note of urgency. Today's picture of Jewish history is completely different from that of forty years ago. It is, for example, still possible to locate film vividly portraying that world which has passed, but the quantity of such films is steadily diminishing. Much of it is being destroyed or its quality is deteriorating until it becomes useless. To save it for posterity, it must be located, copied (in many cases) and kept under proper conditions.

The challenge is not only to the past. Daily, under various auspices, a vast amount of new film is made which will be invaluable for the future researcher and student, as well as the future maker of films on Jewish society. Already such films can be earmarked for preservation.

The Objectives of the Rad Archive

1. *Preservation*   Several years ago, a member of the Hebrew University's New York office was visiting the United Nations and, by chance, discovered that among a consignment of films earmarked for destruction were the proceedings of the historic debate of November 29, 1947, that led to the establishment of the State of Israel. According to United Nations regulations, film material is destroyed after twenty years. At the time, he was able to secure these films and have them transferred to an American Jewish Organization.

Other instances have occurred in which the end has been less than happy. Over the years, the prints of vast numbers of films of Jewish interest have been lost. Today they are, at best, listings in some old trade journal, but no print has been preserved. Every day there is a possibility that valuable films for some reason or another will be destroyed. One of the prime objectives of the Rad Archive is to provide a center where films will be properly and scientifically stored, so that they will be available to future generations who will be able to see for themselves such historic events as the visit of Kaiser Wilhelm II to Palestine in 1898, the East Side of New York at the beginning of the century, Allenby's entry into Jerusalem in 1917, the horrors of Nazi Europe and the hardships of the survivors, the struggle for the Jewish state, Soviet Jews dancing outside the synagogues on Simchat Torah and clandestinely observing Israel Independence Day by celebrations in the woods. They will be able to see films depicting the way of life of Jewish communities which exist no more in pre-war Poland and Lithuania or in Morocco. Or they will be able to see films that have incorporated important aspects of Jewish life and tradition.

In addition, there is a wealth of television material that calls for preservation, ranging from special features on Jewish life or on Israel, that have been shown in many countries, to the newsreel shots that appear almost daily on screens throughout the world. There are also many films made about such outstanding Jewish personalities as David Ben-Gurion, Martin Buber, S.Y. Agnon, and A.J. Heschel, all of which must be brought into the collection so that future generations will be able to see for themselves the immortals of the age.

2. *Reference Center*   Many documentary films, both for cinema and television, are reconstructed on the basis of old footage. Subjects of Jewish and Israeli content are extremely popular with filmmakers, but until now any producer preparing such a film has had to start from scratch and begin to search for available material.

The Rad Archive is being organized to provide detailed information on Jewish film material throughout the world. It is engaged in an ambitious project locating film material of Jewish interest wherever it may be. Such films are to be found under many auspices in film, newsreel and television companies, in archives of all kinds, in the possession of various governments, in the collections of many Jewish organizations, and very often in private hands. All these have to be ferreted out and the maximum information collected for the Rad Archive files. In addition, the Rad Archive is preparing to view the films in its possession for intensive cataloguing, so that it can provide immediate information on any subject covered. Thus, if a producer is contemplating a film about the synagogue, or a researcher is preparing a work on the subject, he would be able to receive prompt information which could list relevant shots in films in the Rad Archive's possession as well as listing films on the subject elsewhere.

The Archive has collected a number of selected feature films, which are of particular value for educational purposes. Movies such as *The Shop on Main Street* and *The Garden of the Finzi-Continis* are shown in connection with the University courses on the "Holocaust." The Yiddish film *Yiddle with a Fiddle* has been preserved for its portrayal of pre-War Jewish life in Eastern Europe now irrevocably gone. Films made in Palestine in the 1930s to show the life of the pioneers and the mood of the country at that period are included in this category.

3. *Research and Education*   The collection of these films is also envisaged as an educational tool. For example, the Hebrew University's Institute of Contemporary Jewry concentrates on teaching the subject of the Jewish world in this century. With the aid of these films, its students will be able not only to read about the communities but to see them and their way of life. Eventually it is hoped that the material collected in the Rad Archive in Jerusalem will serve the wider purposes of education. In the past, Jewish schools have tended to lag in their use of audiovisual aids, but educators are now thinking in terms of extensive film programs. The Rad Archive will be an obvious source when it comes to the preparation of such films, which will help to add a new vitality and dimension to Jewish education.

The Achievements of the Rad Archive

1. *Locating*   The first task undertaken by the Rad Archive has been the locating of relevant film material. Thus far, work has been car-

ried out in two areas, Israel and the United States. The Israeli survey was undertaken directly by the personnel of the Rad Archive. They have so far listed over 1500 films of Israeli and Jewish interest that are available under different auspices in Israel. (This is apart from the rich newsreel clippings in various hands and the great stock of filmed material built up by Israel Television). The Rad Archive has published a catalogue of this material, listing the films and also providing an index giving a breakdown of subject matter.

Parallel to this, a survey has been undertaken in the United States and has appeared under the title *Jewish Films in the United States* (Boston: G.K. Hall, 1976). The Hebrew University reached an agreement with the Cinema Department of the University of Southern California, the latter undertaking responsibility for the direction of this work. Stuart Fox, a graduate student, travelled throughout the United States over the course of a year to search for relevant material. He sought the archives of the major film companies and looked at the libraries of the national television networks. He went through files of old movie magazines, finding pre-World War I reviews of films such as *The Yiddishe Cowboy*. In Washington, he investigated the vast stock of Nazi films being held in the United States. He combed the files of Jewish organizations and examined the Yiddish films available. He also followed leads to private individuals. At the end of his search, he had found information on over 4000 relevant films. In some instances, the references were only in journals, and it is not known if they are still in existence. Some of the many valuable and interesting films are included in this latter group. The invaluable material published has a detailed subject index. Surveys have also been made in various European countries and are scheduled for eventual publication.

2. *Collecting* The Rad Archive has received many valuable collections. One was the complete collection made by the French director Frederic Rossif for his documentary historical film *A Wall in Jerusalem*, which surveys the history of Israel throughout the twentieth century. Rossif worked long on the gathering of material and used only a fraction in his finished film. Now everything is in the Rad Archive.

Another collection received was the material shot for Jules Das-

sin's film *Operation Survival*. Since Dassin went to Israel immediately
after the Six-Day War, his filming reflects the mood and situation of
the country in those historic days. He travelled into Sinai and brought
back a graphic account of the aftermath of war. He visited Israel's
leaders and filmed interviews lasting hours with the late Prime Min-
ister Levi Eshkol, Moshe Dayan and others. Only short sections were
used in the film itself, but all the original footage was turned over to
the Rad Archive.

More recently, a number of important newsreel collections have
been added to the Archive covering events in Israel from the early
1920s to the 1960s. In addition, a number of Jewish organizations
house their films there, including the World Zionist Organization,
the Jewish National Fund and the Joint Distribution Committee.

The Rad Archive is regularly consulted by the filmmakers from
Israel and abroad who are planning films on Jewish and Israeli subjects incorporating documentary material. For example, Israeli television producers regularly consult with the Rad Archive. British
television teams preparing documentaries on Israel worked largely
from the Archive's draft catalogue and the Hollywood producer
Norman Jewison visited Israel to prepare his movie of *Fiddler on the
Roof*. He spent considerable time viewing films illustrating Jewish life
in pre-World War II Eastern Europe, organized for him by the Rad
Archive.

One of the major operations within the Archive is the compilation
of detailed shotlist catalogues to enable the person searching for footage to locate relevant material entry, even when only a few feet might
be involved. Apart from its newsreel collections, a catalogue of holdings of the Archive published in 1976 lists more than a thousand
items.

The Archive has at all times operated on a shoe-string budget
which has prevented it from obtaining many treasures it would wish
to collect. In fact, at the outset there were those who warned against
starting operations with such limited resources. The policy adopted,
however, was that it was better to work in a small way than to leave
the field entirely neglected. A number of proposals to establish Jewish
Film Archives had been made in the past but none has ever been
fruitful. In view of the amount of material that was being lost or was

deteriorating, the decision to go ahead has been justified. The Archive is constantly on the lookout for film material of Jewish significance, even when not professional. Sometimes the film is donated, sometimes it is deposited by the owners who are glad to know that it will be properly preserved. The important thing is that the work is being done and centralized in one major reference center.

THEATER KLANK EN BEELD:
SOUND AND FILM ARCHIVES OF THE DUTCH THEATRE

by Lou Hoefnagels

A theatrical performance cannot be preserved. When the actors have spoken their last lines nothing remains but the memory. And newspaper reviews are proof enough of how widely the descriptions of one and the same performance may differ.

Of course, actors' parts and producers' scripts, stage-set models, costume designs, and photo sequences can all be preserved, but this static material does not fully inform us about what really *happened* on the stage. Theatre is, if it is anything, sound, movement, life.

Today we are fortunate enough to be able to film and tape performances and bring them back to life again at a later date. These records tell us more about the reality of a performance than any subjective description can, although there will, of course, always be a place for the kind of documents and memorabilia traditionally collected by theatrical museums and libraries.

Theater Klank en Beeld, the sound and film archives of theatrical performance in the Netherlands, has been in operation since October 5, 1966. The idea was originally conceived by two theatre buffs. They realized that they would not be able to achieve anything by themselves and presented their plan to the Dutch Actors' Union. The Union greeted it with enthusiasm and called a meeting of representatives of the Theatre Museum, the theatrical companies, radio and television networks, the drama schools, the university departments of drama, the Netherlands Centre of the International Theatre Institute, the record industry, and the Ministry of Culture and Social Affairs.

This assembly, too, warmly welcomed the idea. A four-man committee was formed to investigate all the possibilites. One of the proposals that had been made was that the sound and film archives

Lou Hoefnagels is the founding Director of Theater Klank en Beeld, now part of the Netherlands Theatre Institute.

should not only have historical value for future generations, but also be immediately called into play in attracting audiences from a wider spectrum to the theatre. A role that might, it was appreciated, give rise to problems of copyright.

In 1965 the preparatory committee presented a detailed report. They had taken legal advice, drafted regulations and contracts, found accommodation, made an initial budget estimate, studied ways of financing the venture and the like.

When the new trust was officially created on June 1, 1965, it still had no financial backing. The Theatre Museum had promised part of its basement, and, not long after, the Government offered a $10,000 subsidy for 1966. Two cultural funds gave a total of $23,000 to install a small studio, two listening booths, archives and an office. The actors themselves raised over $3000 for the purchase of the basic equipment. On October 5, 1966, the Archives were declared open by the Minister of Culture and Social Affairs.

The Archives were allotted a dual task: (a) to collect old phonograph records, tapes and films of theatrical performances and (b) to record the best productions of each new season. During the first few years these tasks could be carried out only on a very restricted scale, even though the Archives had already received a great deal of co-operation. All the theatrical companies had written a clause into their contracts to the effect that actors were required to give freely of their services for recordings made for the Archives, and that they would receive no royalties when these recordings were loaned out for non-commercial (i.e. scholarly, artistic or educational) purposes. The Dutch Actors' Union had agreed to these conditions.

At first, however, very few recordings could be made. The Archives had extremely limited financial resources, no technical staff of their own, and were unable to record in stereo. So all recordings had to be commissioned, but that, too, cost money. Still, a start was made in the search for existing recordings. Collectors, actors, the radio and television networks were approached. Phonograph records of plays, revues and monologues were presented to the Archives, and copies were made in the Archives' own studios of material loaned to them. Initially, volunteers undertook this job, but a year was to pass before the Archives were able to employ their own technician.

The first four years were lean ones. The government subsidy rose from $10,000 in 1966 to $28,000 in 1969. Every year there were deficits which the Ministry of Culture and Social Affairs was generous enough to make good. In addition, the Archives received an annual subsidy from the Amsterdam City Council.

It was obvious, however, that if funds were not more rapidly forthcoming, it would be a long time before any reliable record of the current theatrical scene in Holland could be built up. For reasons of economy, the emphasis lay entirely on the making of sound recordings. A number of short films were acquired, either by purchase, co-production, or the copying of television productions, but it was largely a question of making do with whatever happened to be offered or of seizing random opportunities.

In an attempt to stabilize operations the board decided to draw up a five-year plan. The following annual targets of acquisition were set: (a) two medium length films (40-45 mins); (b) five to ten shorter fragments; (c) copies of television plays, to a total length of about ten hours. These films should preferably be in color, but in the majority of cases black-and-white would be adequate. In addition, work should continue on sound recordings and the recording of interviews with old actors, jubilees, farewells and the like. Finally, copies still had to be made of many old films and phonograph recordings of Dutch actors and revue artists, but of this project the end was already in sight.

Of course, the number of recordings to be made would vary from one theatrical season to another, but on the basis of this plan it was possible to convince the Ministry of Culture and Social Affairs that $200,000 a year would be required to finance an effective recording program. Although the purchase of more professional equipment and the engaging of a production manager and two technicians were included in this sum, the actual making of films would still be commissioned.

Since then, the state subsidies have risen considerably. In 1970 a grant was allocated of $57,000, in 1971 of $70,000, in 1972 of $79,000, in 1973 of $88,000, in 1974 of $122,000, in 1975 of $151,000, and for each of the past two years, $186,000.

Small grants have also been obtained from provincial and municipal authorities, while some income is derived from the services Theater Klank en Beeld renders. Even so, in 1975, eighty-six percent of the Archives' running costs were still borne by the state.

Every theatre museum and library has in its collection phono-graph records, tapes and films, but these have usually been acquired more or less by chance and are not lent out. Theater Klank en Beeld, however, very deliberately chooses which productions will find their way into the archives. From the very beginning, a selection commit-tee consisting of a producer, dramaturg, historian, drama critic, and educator have been involved in the making of these decisions.

During the first few years when money was so short, the commit-tee was primarily engaged in deciding which sound recordings should be made. General guidelines were derived from the past experiences of this period. If the opinion of the committee is divided, tape re-cordings will be automatically made of the productions. The com-mittee now spends most of its time on deciding which productions shall be filmed. Decisions concerning the copying of television drama are made in collaboration with a television drama work-group. A committee responsible for selections in the area of revue and musicals has also recently been set up. It goes without saying that the norms governing the decisions made have to be revised from time to time in the light of new movements and trends active in the theatre.

The second remarkable aspect of Theater Klank en Beeld is that tapes and films may be borrowed subject to certain conditions. Visitors to the Archives can, of course, listen to tapes and recordings there, while schools, cultural associations, theatres and other institu-tions can order films by mail. The conditions are that none of the material shall be copied, lent out or exploited commercially. What is important, however, is that this material should be readily available. The theatrical companies, the Dutch Actors' Union, the Copyright Office, all see it as a means of arousing wider interest in the theatre and involving audiences more closely in theatrical life.

Theater Klank en Beeld had been in operation for a year when opportunities for borrowing material were created. Fifty schools availed themselves of this service immediately, even though the choice was at first extremely limited. There are now more than 500 schools, institutions and individuals who make more or less regular use of our tapes and films. For an annual fee they are entitled to borrow as many tapes as they wish. Only the postage has to be paid. Five times a year they receive a bulletin informing them of the new acquisitions. A charge is made for films, but everyone may make use of the rental service, whether he is a registered borrower or not.

Of course, the original recordings are not lent out but stored away in the vaults of the Netherlands Radio Archives. The first working copy is kept in our own archives and from this loan copies are made. Thus, all risk of loss is eliminated. Furthermore, Theater Klank en Beeld is covered by a so-called 'replacement' insurance policy, so that, should our archives be destroyed by fire, we could recopy everything from the originals. A similar system applies for the films, which are kept in the vaults of the Netherlands Film Museum.

Unfortunately, we are not in a position to lend out everything. Most of the copies that have been made of radio and television productions may not leave the archives. Only documentaries and productions for which lending rights have been explicitly granted by the performers and other interested parties can be borrowed.

At first, recordings of theatrical productions were lent out only in their entirety. Later we began to make our own documentary tapes, consisting of a profile of playwrights like Shakespeare, Molière and Chekhov, whose work we have in a variety of versions, together with a number of characteristic scenes. The Theatre Museum subsequently cooperated with us to make color slides to go with the documentary tapes. The theatrical companies have likewise been of great assistance to us in this work.

Since our documentary programs run for forty-five minutes, they are specifically made for classroom use to prepare young people for a visit to the theatre. A careful selection of the filmed fragments is made for inclusion in the planned documentary.

The tapes produced for libraries for the blind present special problems. Such additional information as a description of the stage sets, brief insertions introducing characters as they appear for the first time, and any other relevant details about happenings on the stage are inserted whenever they cannot be deduced from the spoken text.

German, English and French theatrical companies tour Dutch secondary schools by arrangement with the Work and Information Centre for Theatre Education (WIKOR). At the beginning of such a tour, which often lasts for nearly two months, we make a recording, copies of which are then sent to the schools wishing to prepare for the performance. Permission to make such a recording is one of the conditions under which **WIKOR** contracts these companies.

Because our ties with the Theatre Museum are so close, it is only natural that we frequently provide audiovisual material for use at exhibitions held there. The radio and television networks are also beginning to draw on our archives more and more frequently, especially for documentaries, jubilees and the like. As a measure of their respect for our efforts, Dutch television has been donating forty hours of TV drama each year which we are allowed to lend under certain conditions. We received this gift on our tenth anniversary.

Finally, we have already issued three phonograph records of excerpts from works by Dutch authors: one 12-inch LP of a one-man performance and an album containing two LPs with a complete production of a Dutch play.

Theatre Klank en Beeld soon outgrew the basement of the Theatre Museum. Together with the Netherlands Centre of the ITI, it is now located at 166 Herengracht, Amsterdam. In this splendid seventeenth-century house, next door to the Theatre Museum, we have more room for the archives and for the technicians, and even for a small recording studio. Better facilities are also provided for visitors wishing to listen to a play, and there is a small film auditorium seating some eighty persons. The close proximity of museums, library, archives, exhibitions, audio-visual department, and correspondence address for foreign contracts makes it easy for staff to work as a team, and this in its turn is of benefit to the public at large.

Much of the text of this article appeared first in an informative brochure issued in 1976. Lou Hoefnagels was the author and the translator was C. E. Meijer-Jollison of the Netherlands Centre of ITI. Mr. Hoefnagels brought it up to date for this publication.

THE STRATFORD FESTIVAL ARCHIVES

by Daniel W. Ladell

On her first day of work, Margaret Ryerson was shown a dark, cluttered room at the top of the Festival Theatre, given a typewriter and innumerable boxes, and instructed to 'go to it.' This occasion, ten years ago last November, marks the unofficial (and virtually unnoticed) founding of the Stratford Festival Archives. Since that time, what began in a cramped storage room has grown to a collection of well over four hundred cubic feet of material recording every aspect of the development of the most prominent theatre enterprise in Canada. The significance of these Archives as a research resource for the academic community has been evidenced by the dozens of students, authors and professionals who have referred to the collection for help in their particular areas of study. At the same time, however, the Stratford Festival Archives have yet to become widely known.

Perhaps this near anonymity is due to the fact that the Archives did indeed grow from such humble beginnings. The need to preserve the material generated by the Festival was not recognized until 1967, when other institutions first expressed interest in obtaining the theatre's archival material for their own collections. At this time, the Festival Board of Governors decided that the best way to guarantee both the safety and accessibility of important papers and correspondence dealing with the early years was to establish an area at the Festival itself where this material could be properly maintained. A committee was appointed to study the problem and after formal approval of an archival centre at Stratford, the first steps were taken to obtain control of papers and other memorabilia. The task of locating, sorting and cataloguing fell to Mrs. Ryerson, the first archivist.

Mrs. Ryerson spent her first two weeks of employment not at the theatre, but at the home of Tom Patterson, the founder of the Fes-

Daniel W. Ladell is the current Archivist of the Stratford Festival Archives, Canada.

tival. In an upstairs study where she found carton after carton of papers, programs, photographs and personal papers from the first years of the theatre, she began the original task of sorting into general categories.

The only available space where this and more recent material could be catalogued and stored was a storage room at the top of the theatre. While the room was large enough, it was pitifully inadequate in other respects. There were no air vents or heating; the only lights were utility globes hanging from the ceiling; and the single plug on the extension would accommodate either a fan or a heater but unfortunately not both. Some material had already been allotted specific areas on the rough wooden shelves lining the walls. The rest had been stored in stacks of boxes covering the floor and forming a solid wall at one end of the room.

Undismayed, Mrs. Ryerson began the work of collecting the annual posters, programs and other printed material from each season. But while production and publicity records were essentially complete, serious gaps existed in many places. For example, the poster announcing the first season could not be found, except where it had been cut up to use as backing on other material. (A copy of this important poster has still not been located. After all, who in 1953 could have known that there would be another season?) One of the most exciting parts of the job was finding these missing links in sequences of material, especially in the correspondence of Tyrone Guthrie and Cecil Clarke. She prepared lists to coincide with chronological files of letters. Fortunately, to help her in the placing of material, early files from 1953 to 1957 were available, and these she read and assimilated for the accurate picture which they provided of the growth of the Festival from an idea to a permanent theatre structure. Even fifteen years later, she found it impossible not to catch the feelings of elation, panic and challenge associated with this event. And so, during that first year, when the existence of the Archives was unknown even to the Festival people, Mrs. Ryerson continued the gathering, listing and storing of material.

Although a great deal was accomplished towards establishing the permanent archives during this period, Mrs. Ryerson soon found herself increasingly drawn into production work. While the idea persisted, there was little time and less money to spend on the Festival

Archives. It was not until 1971 that interest was renewed.

At this time, when institutions once again began making overtures about acquiring Festival material, the archives project was revived in new quarters with adequate light, space and shelving to insure that the records would be preserved and accessible for reference and research. Although the Archives would have been ideally located in the Festival building, the problems of space arising from a rapidly expanding organization precluded this, and the Archives were located in the Perth Mutual Insurance building a half-block from the theatre, where they remain today.

Since Margaret Ryerson was now working in the production department, in November, 1971, the first of a succession of full-time archivists was hired. Largely because of the efforts of James R. Aikens and Wendy Swain, the Archives have become what they are today. From 1971 to the present, many collections were completed and several new collections, like the complete set of production photographs from 1953 through 1970, were acquired. A card cataloguing system of indexing and cross referencing was also instituted, and steps were taken to publicize the existence of the Stratford Festival Archives, which resulted in a larger influx of researchers and scholars.

Until 1976, the Stratford Festival was the only theatre in Canada with a formally constituted archive, which served to underscore the encompassing creativity of the theatre enterprise. As in all archives, the essential quality remains that of recording not merely achievements of the Festival but also the processes by which they were accomplished. In this way, an ongoing history in as many different aspects as possible is preserved.

Historically, the Stratford Shakespearean Festival represents the first major Canadian theatre company to achieve international status. It is in the Festival Archives that the growth of this theatre to preeminence is recorded. Its theatrical innovations have inspired other theatres around the world. The most immediate example of this is the revolutionary Festival thrust stage, designed by Tanya Moiseiwitsch and Tyrone Guthrie, which allows a 220 degree view by the audience while retaining and augmenting all the adaptability of the traditional proscenium stage. So successful has this stage been that it has served as a direct model for the Guthrie Theatre in Minneapolis and the Crucible Theatre in Sheffield, and has strongly in-

fluenced the design of the Chichester Festival, the Beaumont Theatre at Lincoln Center, the National Arts Centre, and the Olivier
Theatre at the National. Modifications and improvements to the
original design are still being made, the most recent taking place in
1976, when Miss Moiseiwitsch redesigned the originally permanent
balcony to make it movable, presenting new possibilities for staging.
The Festival continues to play a role in developing and redefining the
basic concepts of the audience/performer relationship in modern
theatre.

The success of the Festival speaks for itself, both in terms of
artistic quality and as a business enterprise. Artistically, the Stratford
Festival is recognized as one of the three top-ranking theatres in the
English-speaking world. Its high standards of quality continue to
inspire and invigorate theatre at all levels. Concomitantly as a business venture, the Festival demonstrates by its continued existence
that theatre remains a vital, relevant and necessary medium, capable
of achieving a high degree of self-sufficiency through sheer popularity.

The value of preserving the Festival's records on a continuous
basis becomes doubly important. Like any large scale business enterprise, the Stratford Festival generates prodigious amounts of records
every year. At the same time, the Festival is also, and more impor-
tantly, an artistic enterprise "of great pitch and moment," and the
chronicles of its artistic processes become of vital importance in relation not only to Canadian but also to international theatre. By preserving a full account of the total operation of the Festival, the Archives represents an almost unparallelled resource center. The Archives must concern itself with the disposition of every bit of paper
dealing with every facet of the theatre's operation. For this reason,
the Archives collection is intensive rather than extensive; wherever
possible, records which are submitted are retained in their entirety.

Four major categories of records are preserved: Publicity, Production, Administration, and Special Collections. Each of these
classifications is in turn subdivided to accommodate the divisions
within each department. For example, within the Publicity collection
are maintained separate files of printed material generated by the
Festival, printed material from other theatres, correspondence,
photographs, press clippings, and biographical material.

The collection of printed material produced by the Festival is virtually complete from 1953. Within this category are maintained separate files of house programs for both drama and music, souvenir programs, brochures and other mailing pieces, exhibit catalogues, press releases, publications produced for sale or distribution (such as design folios and postcards), seasonal posters and programs for events which take place within the theatre premises but which have no connection with Festival programs.

Much the same type of publicity material, namely programs, press releases and posters, is maintained in the collection of printed material from other theatres. Among the theatres represented in this collection are Canadian festivals and regional theatres, and prominent foreign theatres like the Guthrie, Royal Shakespeare and National Theatres. The Archives also maintains files of publicity correspondence with the media, advertising agencies, and sponsors, which are transferred intact from the department. Included in these files is research material for publications produced by the publicity department.

A large and comprehensive assortment of photographs represents one of the most valuable of the Publicity collections. These photographs present a complete record of Festival activities from 1953 to 1970. Sub-collections consist of production shots in the form of finished prints and color transparencies, general photographs recording off-stage activity, negatives of photographs whenever obtainable, and miscellaneous non-Festival photographs from various sources used for research, exhibitions, souvenir books and the like.

The press clippings which record the critical success (or failure) of each season from 1953 onwards are preserved in three ways. They are collected into volumes by the publicity department, and into personal scrapbooks donated to the theatre by various individuals. They are also to be found in the complete copies of books and magazines which contain substantial articles on the Festival or related subjects.

The last collection maintained within the larger category of publicity material is composed of individual files on Festival personnel. Included in each file are official biographies, related correspondence, newsclippings, and portrait photographs.

The next major division within the Archives is that of Production. Material in this collection is maintained in nine categories: prompt-

books, scripts of plays produced by the Festival, scripts of plays submitted to but not produced by the theatre, production office files,
individual correspondence, stage management files, design material,
music department files, and workshop files.

The collection of promptbooks is accompanied by other material
as is included with the books when they are transferred from stage
management. Usually there are two books for each production: a
stage manager's book with blocking notes and other stage directions
and a prompter's copy with cues and calls. (There may also be additional books for touring productions.) Any other pertinent documents may be included with them.

Copies containing the actors' annotations, cues or comments are
retained as well as clean copies for duplication purposes. Shooting
scripts for television productions such as *Henry V* and *The Three
Musketeers* are also to be found in the play collection.

The files maintained by the different areas of the production
office is complete from 1956, but there is also a great deal of material
from the early years as well. The most important material in these
files is the correspondence of the artistic director, executive producer,
production manager and others within the department. Individual
files have been created for Tyrone Guthrie, Cecil Clarke, Tanya
Moiseiwitsch, Michael Langham and Tom Patterson among others
because they are so often referred to.

A general collection of material (promptbooks excluded) transferred from stage management is also maintained. Cast lists, scene
breakdowns, rehearsal schedules, production diaries and property
lists are kept separately from such technical material as sound effect
tapes, show music tapes, light cues and layouts, and lighting, sound
and electrical system specifications.

The most valuable records of a production created by the design
department are the original sketches. The Festival is fortunate to
possess a large collection of signed costume sketches representing the
design of nearly every production. For purposes of preservation and
display, they are framed as they are received. Almost as important in
providing a record of the design of a production are a separate collection of wardrobe bibles, with costume construction information,
cloth samples and often reproductions of the original sketches, and a
file of loose sketches from the property and wardrobe departments.

Although many original blueprints are still in use at the theatre, the larger design collection includes floor plans and stage and set sketches for both the Festival and Avon Theatres and the Third Stage. Augmenting this material is a collection of models, props and constructions. These set and stage models and certain other significant properties or wardrobe items, such as the memorable set of masks from the 1954-1955 production of *Oedipus Rex*, complete the design collection.

The music department comprises the other major department within Production. Play and opera scores, music promptbooks, and a complete file of correspondence including that of the music director regarding concerts, master classes and opera productions from 1953 to the present comprise this sub-collection.

In 1965, the Festival inaugurated a program of seasonal workshops with the specific aim of developing and augmenting the skills of actors within the company. The Archives maintains the files of these workshops, which may include promptbooks for workshop productions as well as other material on voice, movement and special technical class.

The business records of the Festival are collectively maintained under the classification of Administration. With the theatre's administrative complex are five smaller departments: the administrative office proper, the Board of Governors, the accounting office, the fund raising office, and the box office. The records pertaining to each are kept independently.

The administrative office retains for its own use the most recent ten years of material. Correspondence and other files prior to the ten year period are transferred to the Archives, where they are preserved exactly as they are received.

The Board of Governors produces three types of records. The first is a general file of the minutes of the Full Board and annual meetings, together with related reports and correspondence. A second separate category is maintained for the minutes and correspondence of the various committees of the Board. Lastly, the President's and other annual reports are filed chronologically.

Five categories of records are produced by the accounting department. These are ledgers and journals, audited financial statements, periodic statements, budgets and projections, and payroll and pension records. Like administrative files, these are retained for a period of time before being transferred, in this case for seven years.

Material relating to early campaigns comprises the fund raising office files. This material includes membership reports, campaign correspondence, brochures and other mailing material, mailing lists and statements of procedure.

The remaining Administrative category is the box office, the files of which consist of box office reports, statements and lists, records of attendance, and a very limited amount of correspondence.

By far the most intriguing and diversified material maintained in the Archives is found in the Special Collections. All material not directly generated by the Festival in the course of its operation, but which is preserved for reasons of commemorative or aesthetic value or for reference, is placed in this category.

The largest special collection embraces films, videotapes and microfilms produced either for reference purposes or to record some particular aspect of the theatre's history of activities. Films include *The Stratford Adventure* produced by the National Film Board and *The Players,* a documentary of the 1974 Australian tour of *The Imaginary Invalid.* The collection of videotapes consists primarily of complete recordings made of productions, beginning with *Tartuffe* in 1968 and continuing to the present, although there are also a few miscellaneous items such as a copy of the CTV videotape of the 1966 television version of *Henry V.* The microfilm library is comprised of prints duplicating every promptbook from 1953 through 1970. These films were made to take the place of the fragile originals in research and reference.

A great many items donated to the theatre especially during the early years are preserved in a large collection of commemorative material and Shakespeareana. The collection of commemorative material includes official greetings and congratulations, and certificates, plaques and medallions presented to the Festival. In the collection of Shakespeareana are badges and medals celebrating Shakespeare's Jubilee in 1759 and other important anniversaries, a copy of the Fourth Folio, prints and engravings of famous actors and scenes from the plays, and scholarly works, among which are those written during the great Cryptogram controversy.

The most valuable artifact is the Glastonbury Chair, which was donated to the Festival in 1958 by an American collector. This Tudor oak chair, which dates from the early sixteenth century, has for centuries been reputed to have been Shakespeare's, and has a fully documented history dating from the eighteenth century. Even if its authenticity as a Shakespearean relic is unverifiable, its close connection with the scandal surrounding young Ireland's Shakespearean forgeries (it is said to have inspired them!) makes it an interesting and valuable article of memorabilia. The last category within this collection consists of items of significance in the history of Canadian and European theatre, such as production files, scrapbooks, programs, playbills and posters.

The major purpose of the Archives remains the preservation of material, preferably in the same order as it is received. Services to outside users is never allowed to take precedence over this primary responsibility. But at the same time these records represent an invaluable source of reference and information for Festival personnel and an important center of study for students and scholars in many disciplines. So, while the Archives continue to help make Stratford's contribution to Canadian theatre and to the Shakespearean tradition an enduring one, it has always been hoped that side by side with the working theatre an active center of research and scholarship could be developed.

At this time steps are being taken to realize this objective. Several months ago, Robin Phillips, the Artistic Director of the Festival, announced plans for a new building to be constructed adjoining the present Avon Theatre. The extension, christened Stage One, will house a theatre academy as well as an additional performance space for experimental productions. It will "be so designed and built—in terms of outlets and proportions—that with the addition of technological equipment, it can serve both as a television and a film studio."

This is a revolutionary leap forward not only in the growth of the Festival but in the development of Canadian theatre as well. And, as the role of the Stratford Festival changes, so must the functions and objectives of its Archives. With the opening of Stage One in 1979, the Festival Archives must be ready to exceed its strict technical functions and become an active and useful center for research of all kinds. At the same time, preparations will have to be made to accommodate an even greater annual volume of material.

The Archives will continue to preserve the important records of each season and to document fully the unique artistic achievement of the Festival. In addition, with the recent integration of the theatre's research office and the archives, the foundation for a basic research center has already been established. By strengthening this concept over the next few years, a resource base can be created which will become of inestimable value in meeting the research needs of both Stage One and the academic community.

The Archives has come a long way from the time when the only justification for its existence was the establishment of a storage area to house theatre records. Today, the Archives has succeeded in becoming an efficient, permanent archival center where material will be properly maintained. But much still remains to be done if the Archives is to meet the second and greater challenge of transforming itself from a musty storeroom into an active, vital, functioning theatre resource. It is towards the accomplishment of this goal that the future development of the Stratford Festival Archives will be directed.

THE SHAKESPEARE CENTRE LIBRARY

by Wendy Warnken

Situated next to Shakespeare's birthplace on Henley Street, Stratford-upon-Avon, the Shakespeare Centre Library is a perfect blend of place and subject, as well as a symbol of the great poet's influence throughout the world. The Centre was opened in 1964 to commemorate the 400th anniversary of Shakespeare's birth and during the past fourteen years it has been most successful in carrying out what it considers to be the main reason for its existence, the preservation and maintenance of the Shakespearean properties and the general advancement of Shakespearean knowledge.

The Shakespeare Birthplace Trust and the Shakespeare Memorial Theatre began collecting materials at relatively the same time in the nineteenth century, developing separate but complementary collections of manuscripts, books, pictures, and theatrical items. In 1947, the two libraries were brought under the direction of the Director of the Birthplace Trust with the two collections merging in 1964 to become the Shakespeare Centre Library.

There are approximately 30,000 books, pamphlets and periodicals in the Library, with 400 of the earliest items including *The Grete Herball* (1529), *The Chronicles of Holinshed* (1577), Cinthio's *Hecatommithi* (1580) and the *Works* of Ben Jonson (1616). There is a comprehensive collection of sixteenth and seventeenth century items, all relating to Shakespeare, either by their availability to the dramatist, or as sources for other Elizabethan literature. His contemporaries are well accounted for, as well, but, understandably, the focus of the collection rests with Shakespeare himself. The numerous editions include all four folios of the seventeenth century, the early quartos, and later complete editions, ranging from Rowe, Pope and Johnson to the modern Arden, Penguin and Cambridge. While the texts themselves represent the cornerstone of the collection, there is a wealth of critical analysis and historical accounts of theatrical

Wendy Warnken is Archivist of the Theatre and Music Collection of the Museum of the City of New York.

development and techniques. Elizabethan and Jacobean life is illuminated through books and pamphlets on education, travel, medicine and crafts as well as topographical studies of Warwickshire.

The Library's extensive collection of Shakespearean texts and criticisms is impressive, of course, but what makes the Library unique is the holdings acquired from the Royal Shakespeare Theatre and the Shakespeare Memorial Theatre. There are photographs from practically every Shakespearean production done in Stratford, 15,000 in all. The Centre can also accommodate the oversized (up to five feet) blow-ups used for modern publicity purposes.

Programs from every production are kept in specially-made folders, along with reviews, tickets and newspaper clippings. There is a complete collection of costume sketches from Royal Shakespeare Company productions, dating from 1961 when the Company was created to the present. Set and costume design from Shakespeare Memorial productions of the 1950s to 1961 are also available to researchers.

Promptbooks, in extraordinarily good condition, range from Henry Irving's *Hamlet* and several of John Philip Kemble's productions to every RSC show, including show work done in Stratford, London and on worldwide tour.

Music, an important element in most RSC productions, is preserved in manuscript form and there are recordings of most of Shakespeare's plays.

One of the most fascinating parts of the RSC holdings is the 93 scrapbooks which have been yearly put together, recording the major and, occasionally, minor happenings at the Theatre. One can spend hours looking through just one volume, since each, approximately 20" x 15" in size, is literally bulging with documentation of the plays and players comprising each of the seasons at Stratford and London. One can read every review, article, interviews with and articles by the actors, directors and designers involved in a particular play. Even the domestic entanglements of marriage, birth and death are recorded. These scrapbooks are created with the sort of thoroughness and extreme care which can only be achieved by people who are intimately concerned with a particular company's work and personnel. To avoid anyone wondering if the scrapbooks connote nothing more than a rather sophisticated level of gossip, it should be noted that they contain a wealth of material which would be difficult for any researcher to locate individually. If one, for instance, were to do some research on Harold Pinter, one would have to go to several of these volumes, as the RSC has produced six of his plays. In addition to the reviews not reprinted elsewhere, there are items which have been printed solely by the RSC, including a previously unpublished short story by Pinter.

The scrapbooks are also an excellent way to note the development and growth both of the Company as a unit and of the individual artists who are the sustaining force of the RSC.

All the Library's materials can be found in alphabetical order. There is a RST Persons Index which lists all actors, directors, designers *et al* associated with the Shakespeare Memorial Theatre and the RSC from circa 1947 onwards. The RST Plays Index lists all productions staged by the Shakespeare Memorial Theatre between 1879-1960 and the RSC since 1961.

The Centre Library has a very handsome reading room seating fifteen readers, but when necessary can accommodate more. Seminar facilities are available in the annex next door and the Centre's basement level has adequate room for microfilm, recording and typing equipment. Photocopying is possible, and anything read at the Centre can be reproduced by photography.

To use the reading room, there are no charges or special requirements. If you will need more than three days, the Library issues a ticket upon receipt of a letter of recommendation. It is requested that you write in advance, stating your interest and needs. The Library has a small but extremely knowledgeable and accommodating staff, and is open year round.

THEATRE RESEARCH IN MOSCOW AND LENINGRAD

by Micky Levy

The creative spirit of Russian theatre artists has long been a source of wonder and speculation to the people of the United States. Since the Revolution, with the emergence of a national Russian theatre, American authorities such as Norris Houghton and Lee Strasberg have made pilgrimages to this theatrical mecca and have whetted the appetites of many of us eager to know more about the exotic, the experimental, and the exciting in Soviet theatre. In fact, it is probably due to their initial reporting back in the 1930s that the present generation of theatre researchers first became familiar with the names of Meyerhold and Tairov.

Along with those who have reported so vividly about the dramatic wonders in Moscow and Leningrad, there have also been others with tales of frustrated attempts at research into the distinguished artistic heritage which is documented and stored in the vast libraries and repositories in the Soviet Union.

According to Patricia Kennedy Grimstead, whose book *Archive and Manuscript Repositories in the USSR* was most helpful in preparing this report, "Archival research possibilities are extremely limited for scholars not associated with one of the exchange programs." Those of us with a sleuthing instinct are usually spurred on by such a challenge.

In a familiar library in our own country we have all undergone an occasional tense moment due to a "tucked-away" manuscript or an evasive clipping. Different standards, rules, language and alphabet can cause confusion or present a real obstacle in a foreign country. But the bonds that tie theatre people of the world together tend to include theatre librarians. This is also true in the Soviet Union.

The large state libraries and museums which appear impersonal because of their size usually have highly qualified specialists who will assist the foreign researcher. The smaller "apartment" museums and

Micky Levy is a specialist in Soviet theatre and has done extensive research in the collections she describes.

libraries are tended by people who are familiar with all of the facts and facets of the life of their particular subject and are more than willing to impart their knowledge.

Planning in advance is probably the most important single bit of advice for the scholar who intends research. Many of the difficulties can be avoided by making prior arrangements. Correspondence which states credentials, the purpose of the work, precise reference to the type of documents required and the time and duration of the visit should be taken care of many months in advance. Letters requesting information of the necessary requirements for entrance should be sent registered.

The basis of a successful interchange should be understanding and good manners, both of which are helpful in any situation, in any country. The scholar should also be aware that rules in the Soviet Union are not made to be broken and any requests for exceptions will not be warmly received. Many theatre libraries appear almost grateful that someone wants to share their special interest and have been known to extract unknown materials for perusal, to bring as a gift a valuable bit of memorabilia or to suggest an alternate plan.

The availability of copying machines in the United States has caused us to forget the hours of painstaking copying that was common in the past. In the Soviet Union these machines are not available, and although photographic services exist, one must obtain permission and allow time for copying. The cost is quite minimal.

No visit to the USSR for theatre research would be complete without visiting the USSR Center of the International Theatre Institute where Mr. Valery Khasanov, the Consult-in-Chief and able theatre writer and translator, cordially assists those in need. Special thanks are due to him and his staff for updating and revising this article for publication and to the directors of all of the libraries for their valuable contributions.

MOSCOW

A.A. Bakhrushin State Central Theatrical Museum
Address: Bakhrushin Ulitsa 31/12 Moscow 113054
Hours: Daily 12:00 noon to 7:00 p.m. except Tuesdays and first
    Monday of each month.
Director: F.K. Shaporin

Founded in 1894 by A.A. Bakhrushin, this is the oldest and largest Soviet theatrical museum. Collection of more than 100,000 items dates from late nineteenth and early twentieth centuries. Personal collections of well-known theatre directors, dramatists, actors, critics, designers, composers, and administrators abound.

Special section contains collection on theatres, theatre journals, autographs, playbills, tickets, scrapbooks, etc. Over 250,000 photographs and negatives as well as manuscripts, books, posters, iconography, models, souvenirs and relics. Permanent exhibition of history of national theatre, travelling exhibition, lectures, guided tours. Photographs and negatives of theatrical productions are catalogued and available for viewing.

The well-trained staff is most helpful to foreign scholars but adequate identification is required and an appointment in advance will assure readiness of materials in the small reading room. The stacks are not open but each division has a card catalogue.

This library is under the jurisdiction of the Ministry of Culture and it is suggested that contact be made with them for information.

Library of the All-Russia Theatre Association (*VTO*)
Address: Gorky Street 16/2 Moscow K-9
Hours: 10:00 a.m. to 6:00 p.m. except Saturday and Sunday.
Chairman: Mikhail Tsarev

This is probably the single, most important source for theatre historians in Moscow and Leningrad. The VTO gives concrete, practical help to professionals in acting, directing, staging, etc. It organizes exhibitions of scenography and theoretical conferences on problems of theatrical processes. It has a large staff of highly qualified experts in all branches of theatre. Also connected with the VTO are factories that produce scenery, make-up, props and other technical equipment of theaters.

The library has a rich collection of Soviet and foreign books and its archives contains photos, posters, press clippings, and all documents concerning most productions in all Soviet theatres and outstanding foreign productions.

The USSR Center of the International Theatre Institute is located at the same address and Mr. Valery Khasanov is a most able and willing contact for information regarding entrance to any collections as well as current theatre information in Soviet theatres. As Consult-in-Chief, he can aid in gaining entrance to the VTO. Since special documents are required for many of the libraries, it is suggested that correspondence with Mr. Khasanov be made well in advance. In Moscow, the phone number is 229-3039.

Central State Archives of Literature and Art (*TsGALI*)
Address: Leningrad Highway 50, Moscow 12512
Hours: 8:30 a.m. to 5:00 p.m.
Director: N. B. Volkova

Formerly the Central State Literary Archive. The collection is housed in a specially constructed building less than thirty minutes from central Moscow and contains literature, theatre, ballet, music, and cinema manuscripts as well as visual art material such as sculpture, architecture and painting. Each section contains the personal collection of a single important figure. Another section houses special collections dealing with persons whose main archives are located elsewhere, such as the Pushkin or Tolstoy collections. It maintains information on theatre archives, museums, artistic publications, government artistic committees and organizations, unions, societies of actors, directors, composers, and designers as well as academies and educational institutions in the arts.

The staff handles individual requests from extensive catalogues. The reading room contains an alphabetical list of individuals with dates of materials and number of storage units. Much fragile material is microfilmed. Microfilm and photo requests are accepted. Comprehensive published guides to the artistic division covers all materials and it is suggested that the researcher study this before entrance.

Central Theatre Library
Address: Moscow, 8/1 Pushkin Street
Hours: Daily except Sunday and last day of the month from
   11:00 a.m. to 8:00 p.m. Closed July and August.
Director: Mrs. L. A. Bykovskaia

Founded 1921 at Maly State Academic Theatre, the collection contains 220,000 volumes of books and periodicals, 350,000 press clippings and more than 60,000 photographs, post cards, etc.; primarily on drama, dramatic theory and criticism. There are card catalogues available for Russian and foreign books. There is also a subject card catalogue of drama, ballet, costume, Russian and foreign periodicals. Photographic service with director's permission. No typing on premises.

Moscow Art Theatre Museum

Address: Proezd Khudozhestvennogo Moscow 103846
Hours: Tuesday, Wednesday and Friday, 1:00 to 8:00 p.m. (In summer, 11:00 a.m. to 6:00 p.m.). Thursday, Saturday and Sunday, 11:00 a.m. to 6:00 p.m. Reading room open Tuesday, Wednesday, Friday and Saturday, 11:00 a.m. to 5:00 p.m. Closed Monday.
Director: P. P. Kabanov

Founded in 1923 for the express purpose of preserving materials concerning the activities of the Art Theatre. Permanent exhibition concerning the lives of the founders and the main stages of theatre work in the past and present is on display.

Nemirovitch-Danchenko Museum

(Affiliated with the Moscow Art Theatre Museum)
Address: Nemirovitch-Danchenko Street, Moscow
Hours: Wednesday and Thursday, Noon to 7:00 p.m.; Friday, Saturday and Sunday, 11:00 a.m. to 6:00 p.m. Closed Monday and Tuesday.

Located in the flat where V. I. Nemirovitch-Danchenko lived during the last five years of his life. Memorial rooms include bedroom, his cabinet, dining room and small living room where the museum exhibition is displayed.

Collection contains family memorabilia, information on his life and work with the Moscow Art Theatre, photographs of great Russian artists presented to him, private papers and his library.

Stanislavsky Museum

(Affiliated with Moscow Art Theatre Museum)
The Museum is closed for restoration. Opening planned for October 1978
Address: Stanislavsky Street 6, Moscow 6
Director: P. P. Kabanov

The Museum is the house in which Stanislavsky lived and died. Rooms preserved as memorials are his bedroom, his cabinet, his dining room, the rooms where rehearsals took place, a hall with the stage where performances were given, the rooms of Maria Lilina, actress of Moscow Art Theatre and wife of Stanislavsky.

The collection contains only materials related to the artist's life and work: photographs of his childhood and adolescence, early acting photographs, scene and costume designs and production sketches, stage models, books, programs, posters, and press clippings. Most of his director's scripts and archives are in the Moscow Art Theatre Museum. Visitors may photograph with permission. Permanent exhibition halls are used to show materials relating to Stanislavsky's life as an artist, producer, teacher and theoretician of acting.

V. I. Lenin State Library with the Order of Lenin
Address: Kalinin Prospect 3, Moscow
Hours: Reading Room: 9:00 a.m. to 10:00 p.m. except the
    last Monday of the month. All other departments closed
    Saturday and Sunday.

Every book and academic dissertation published in the Soviet Union is contained in this library of over twenty million volumes. Originally established in 1862 in the Pashkov Palace, the present building was erected after the Revolution and faces the Kremlin. While not specifically a theatre library, it represents a most important resource. General card catalogue, paging and catalogue search service are available for foreign scholars. Detailed subject catalogue and abstracts of dissertations are available. Special permission is required for reading of dissertations. Staff of specialists offers willing assistance.

Bolshoi Theatre Museum
Address: Moscow, Swerdlov Square
Hours: Open by appointment with the director and before
    and during performances.

Founded in 1920, the museum contains scene sketches, plans for productions and costume designs for operas and ballets. The collection also includes letters, autographs and photographs of opera and ballet performers. Original sketches by Korovin, Benois and Federovski are here preserved.

Museum of the Maly Theatre
Address: Swerdlov Square 1/6 Moscow
Hours: Daily during performances. Closed during July and August.
Director: E. M. Strutinskaya

Founded in 1927 by the Theatre Administration, the holdings relate to the history of the theatre. The collection includes photographs and negatives of the actors in life and in their parts as well as programs, clippings, set and costume sketches, manuscripts, prints, drawings, sculpture, paintings, portraits and production information. Complete card catalogue is available. No photographs are permitted except by staff photographer.

Tours of exhibition and anniversary exhibitions are found in the main lobby of the theatre.

Museum of the State Academic Vakhtangov Theatre
Address: Arbat 24/26 Moscow
Hours: Daily during performances and by appointment.
Director: I. L. Sergeeva

Founded in 1913 as the Third Studio of the Moscow Art Theatre, the holdings were not organized as a museum until 1923. Contains compilations of manuscripts, press releases, scores, stage photographs, set and costume designs, elevations, drawings and posters for each production. A catalogue exists of actors and directors, roles played, productions, clippings, etc. Material is available on Vakhtangov and his early students as well as production committee reports.

The museum prepares temporary and traveling exhibitions. Typewritten copies of documents are available upon request at a fee.

LENINGRAD

Leningrad State Theatrical Museum
Address: 6 Ostrovski Place, Leningrad, 191011, Phone 211 8623
Hours: Daily (except Tuesday) 12:00 noon to 7:00 p.m. Reference
    room open Wednesdays and Fridays 12:00 noon to 5:00 p.m.
    Special collections closed Saturdays and Sundays.
Director: I. V. Evstigneeva

Founded in 1918, the Museum has one of the nation's largest collections of theatre history material. Included are the collections of the Alexandrinski, Maikhailovski and Marinski Theatres, set and costume designs from A.V. Lunacharskii's library, the M.G. Savina home-museum collection, the V.V. Protopov collection and many well-known artists such as Gorbounov; Chaliapin, Komissarzhevskaia, and Solov'ev.

The painting section contains pre-Revolution set designers such as Golovine, Vasnetzov, Korovin, Bakst and others as well as Soviet set designers Akimov, Bobychov, Dimitriev, Konstantinovski. The cinema section deals only with stage actors who performed in motion pictures.

The sound library collection contains songs and monologues of Russian artists before the Revolution and songs, monologues and scenes from Soviet and foreign musicals and plays.

Photographs authorized by the Administration will be taken by the Museum's photo studio.

Library of the Leningrad Branch of VTO
Address: Nevsky Prospect 86, Leningrad 191025, Phone 212 4479
Hours: 1:00 p.m. to 6:00 p.m. Saturday 1:00 p.m. to 4:00 p.m.
    Closed Sunday.
Director: Marina Yuzefovna Komarova

The Library was established by the merging of the Palace of Artistic Workers and the All-Russian Theatre Society (VTO) and maintains a circulating library and reading room. It contains hand-written and typed materials from personal archives, clippings, musical scores and stenotypes of theatrical conferences. Special permission is required and identification from university must be submitted before the reading room may be used.

Lunacharskii State Theatrical Library
Address: Division of Manuscripts Zodchego Rossi Ulitsa 2,
    Leningrad 191011. Phone 210 9383
Hours: Daily 11:00 a.m. to 7:00 p.m. and Saturdays 11:00 a.m. to
    4:00 p.m. Closed Sunday.
Director: N.V. Piatkova

Manuscript division pertains to pre-revolutionary Russian theatre. It includes prompt copies of all plays produced in Russia from 1756 to 1917, plays in foreign languages performed in theatres from sixteenth to nineteenth century, and personal correspondence of theatre people. Another division contains set and costume designs and production sketches. Formerly the library of the Imperial Thea-

tres, it contains more than 350,000 books and manuscripts.
Photographs are permitted. The library maintains a photographic studio.

State Ethnographic Museum of the People of the USSR
Address: Enginerhaya Ulitsa 4/1 Leningrad, 191011. Phone 211 3101
Hours: Daily from 11:00 a.m. to 7:00 p.m. Ticket office open until
    6:00 p.m. Closed Mondays. Admission card required.
Director: I.I. Baronova
Science Secretary: L.N. Molotova

The Museum houses ethnographical material on 130 folk groups
of the U.S.S.R. and contains puppet theatres of different national
traditions, folklore theatres, ritual scenes, costumes, designs for stage
plays; and maquettes. In special collections are materials of expeditions including texts, photos, descriptions and recordings. Museum
photographic service is available.

Circus Museum
Address: Fontanka 3, Leningrad, 196011. Phone 210-4413
Hours: Daily (except Saturday and Sunday) 11:00 a.m. to 5:00
    p.m.
Director: A.Z. Levin

The collection contains more than 1760 books in Russian and
1180 in foreign languages. Pamphlets, photographs, programs,
posters, drawings and memorabilia which covers three hundred years
of circus. Photographs of famous acrobatic acts are accompanied by
diagrams of procedures for their reconstruction for reference and
scholarly research. Permanent exhibition of public spectacles and
related subjects is on display.

The museum was established in 1929 and is unique in the USSR.
It reflects the history of Russian, Soviet and foreign circus art and
collects everything that is connected with the subject.

Central Music Library of Kirov State Academic Theatre
    of Opera and Ballet
Address: Ulitsa Zodchego Rossi, 2, Leningrad 191011.
    Phone 216-8463
Hours: 11:00 a.m. to 3:00 p.m. daily; 11:00 a.m. to 2:00 p.m.
    Sundays. Closed Mondays.

Collection from St. Petersburg Imperial Theatre. Operas and

ballet musical scores, partituras, librettos, handbooks and music magazines. Large collection of handwritten letters of Russian and foreign composers of the nineteenth and twentieth centuries. All scores and librettos are covered in one of two card catalogues. The other covers letters and autographs.

Most theatres in Leningrad have their own literature departments and museums which contain press releases, photographs, negatives, programs and scripts. Below is a listing of some of the more prominent ones.

Gorky Theatre
Address: Fontanka 65, Leningrad 191023. Phone 210-2400
Museum Director: A.E. Yahnin

Pushkin Academic Dramatic Theatre
Address: Ostrovsky Plaza, Leningrad 19011. Phone 210-2239
Director: M.L. Vivien

Kirov Academic Theatre of Opera and Ballet
Address: Theatre Plaza 1, Leningrad 190000. Phone 216-0016
Director: A.N. Saharova

Maly Academic Opera Theatre Museum
Address: Art Plaza 1 Leningrad, 191011. Phone 210-3744
Director: K.N. Liphart

Academic Comedy Theatre
Address: Nevsky Prospect 56 Leningrad 191011. Phone 214-0611
    Ext. 11
Director: T.D. Zolitnitskaya

Bolshoi Puppet Theatre
Address: Nekrasova Ulitsa 10, Leningrad 192194. Phone 272-1713
Director: J.G. Tsionsky

Theatre of Young Spectators
Address: Pioneer Plaza 1, Leningrad 196126. Phone 210-0072.
    Ext. 2813
Director: E.M. Romanovskaya

Leningrad contains a wealth of information on the story and practice of theatre. Below are additional sources including archival materials that may be useful to the scholar.

Department of Manuscripts of the Leningrad Public Library in the name of Schedrina.
Address: Sadovaya Ulitsa 18, Leningrad 191011. Phone 218-0191

Manuscript, newspaper and magazine departments and reading rooms of the Library of the Academy of Sciences of the USSR
Address: Birjevaya Ulitsa 1, Leningrad 199164. Phone 218-3592

Science Library of the Institute of Theatre, Music and Cinematography.
Address: Plaza of St. Isaacs Cathedral #5. Phone 215-9348

Archives of State Russian Museum.
Materials on the art of stage decoration and costumes.
Address: Enginerhaya 4/2, Leningrad 191011. Phone 214-7344

Archives of the State Hermitage.
Theatre and stage decoration and painting of the eighteenth century.
Address: Dvortsovaya 34-36, Leningrad 191065. Phone 212-9510.

THEATRE RESEARCH RESOURCES IN WEST BERLIN

by Paul S. Ulrich

Prior to World War II Berlin had many institutions with material for theatre research: the Prussian State Library (Preussische Staatsbibliothek), the libraries of the Society for Theater History (Gesellschaft für Theatergeschichte), the Theater Institute of the Friedrich Wilhelm University, the Association for the History of Berlin (Verein fur die Geschichte Berlins), the Prussian State Theater (Preussisches Staatstheater) with the Louis Schneider Theater Collection, the Art Library (Kunstbibliothek) with the Lipperheide Costume Library, the numerous theatres with their files and archives and a theatre lending library, as well as numerous private collections. At war's end, the situation appeared dismal. In addition to the war-caused loss of the museum of the Prussian State Theater and a large percentage of the holdings of the Society for Theater History and the Association for the History of Berlin, the Nazi "purification" of library holdings of Jewish and anti-Nazi writers had already removed much valuable material from the public collections. A further dispersion resulted from emigration and the ideological and political division of Germany.

Even though many of the war losses were irreplaceable, the situation today is much better. Several institutions have made an effort to collect material on the theatre, particularly the Berlin theatre, which has often produced holdings accumulated in a pack rat-like fashion and lacking a definite concept in the hope that the mere accumulation of anything obtainable will somehow make up for the losses already sustained. Unfortunately, even in the recent past some losses have occurred: the archive of Dr. Robert Steinfeld, which dates back to 1920 and which was a treasure chest of information for theatre research, was sold to the Theater Institute in Cologne following Dr. Steinfeld's death in April, 1957. Although the various theatres have small reference libraries with play scripts, their

Paul Ulrich, an American, is now a librarian at the Amerika-Gedenkbibliothek in Berlin.

archives are generally stored in such a manner as to be more a hindrance than a help to research.

Various reference works on libraries and academic institutions have much information on the respective holdings, but often even this information does not give a clear indication of what the researcher can expect to find. This report therefore presents the historical development of these institutions in order to convey a better understanding of what is present in West Berlin, how it is arranged and how it can be used.

Walter Unruh Theater Historical Collection
(Theaterhistorische Sammlung Walter Unruh)
Riemeisterstr. 21-23, 1000 Berlin 37

This collection, a donation of Walter Unruh (1880-1961), the "Danziger Lachs" liqueur company director, to the city of Berlin, has been placed on permanent loan with the Theater Institute of the Free University. It is housed in the basement of the Institute and is supervised by a theatre student. As a result of numerous moves and the lack of continuous supervision, there is no central catalogue of the holdings, although some of the material has been catalogued.

Begun about 1920, this collection of books, autographs and playbills was well known to Berlin theatre researchers even before the war, and it served Unruh as a source for various articles and books on the theatre. In September 1945, Unruh gave this collection to the city of Berlin in the hopes that it would serve as the basis for a future theatre research collection and museum.

At this time, the library had more than 8000 volumes and was organized into fifteen divisions, among them: drama, dramaturgy, directing, theatres of individual cities and biographies, with many of the divisions being further subdivided. The playbill collection had over 10,000 pieces, including several of the oldest German theatre announcements. In addition, there were thousands of autographs, letters, cards and role photos as well as numerous curiosities.

Following the political turmoil in 1949, which resulted in a division of the city administration, the West sector took over the administration of the collection. During the move of the collection to a side wing of the Charlottenburg Castle in 1950, all but 200 of the particularly valuable playbills were lost. Over the next two years,

Unruh made donations of books on the theatre plus books and periodicals from the estate of the playwright and dramaturg Rudolf von Gottschall (1823-1909). Writings, photos and other objects were obtained from the estate of the actress Adele Sandrock (1863-1937).

On December 15, 1953, the collection, renamed the "Walter Unruh Theater Historical Collection," was placed on permanent loan with the Theater Institute of the Free University. At this time it consisted of 8000 volumes, a picture collection of about 13,000 items, 8000 autographs, about 200 playbills, a newspaper clipping collection and the furniture which had been purchased for the Collection. Later, Unruh donated two cartons containing the estate of the playwright and theatre director Paul Linsemann (1871-19?) to the Collection.

During the negotiations with the Theater Institute, Unruh described in a short report how his collection developed:

At first I only collected books of theatre content.

Ferdinand Strassow gave me a number of nice letters from artists and writers. This gift formed the basis of the autograph collection.

From Baron von Biedermann I received a large number of playbills (primarily from Dresden) and built up a playbill collection around it.

From Albert Berthold in Berlin I got the handwritten resume of Josef Nesper (1844-1929) together with many letters written to him by many artists, plus about thirty letters from the Duke of Meiningen and the Baroness. Through Berthold I was also able to get a large number of letters written to the Court Councillor (Ludwig) Raupp (1845-1931) in Berlin, including many written instructions from the Duke of Meiningen to Raupp.

From the second-hand bookdealer Martin Breslauer in Berlin I was able to buy very cheaply a large number of letters written to the Dresden theatre director (Josef) Ferdinand Nesmuller (1818-1895) — certainly more than a hundred.

With the help of the above mentioned Berthold I also bought from Mrs. Raupp the sketchbook of the Duke of Meiningen. It contained about 150 figures which were drawn by the Duke himself.

From Mrs. Toni Tetzlaff I received sketches made by her father, the Regisseur Carl Tetzlaff (1837-1914) of Vienna and Berlin (September 1940).

Christmas 1940 I received from Bernard Salomon the estate of the actor Ernst Gettke (1841-1912). It contained many informative letters on the founding of the Stage Union.

Napoleon Kaps from Weimar, Seebach-Stift, whom I got to know through his boarding house friend Wilhelm Rontz, gave me a number of photos of artists, primarily from the early years.

On September 28, 1942, the Intendant Councillor and Regisseur Albert Hugelmann from Danzig gave me twenty-four pictures of Alexander Girardi (1850-1918) and two. . .of Adele Sandrock.

From Mrs. Thielscher I received a plaster medal of Richard Alexander (1852-1923), thereafter eleven pictures of her husband Guido Thielscher (1859-1941).

During a visit to Danzig in September 1942, the character actor Walter Loderer of the Danzig State Theater gave me a number of his role pictures.

In November 1942 I obtained over 170 photo postcards of members of the Danzig State Theater from the years 1900 to 1910 (my friend Eugen Rogorsch discovered them in the Olivaer Postcard Store). I likewise received from Erich Gilka over sixty pictures of artists which had formerly hung in the restaurant of his father.

On November 28 Max Witt gave me (as he had so often before) a very large number of film artists (almost 300 photos).

My friend Erich Friedlander in Hermsdorf gave me on December 13, 1942 about 200 artists postcards of members of the former Royal Theater in Berlin.

In his will, the actor Albert Bassermann (1867-1952) left his estate, which was stored in the Zurich Playhouse, to the city of Berlin. The Walter Unruh Theater Historical Collection was deemed the logical place to deposit this estate and on October 14, 1954, it arrived at the Theater Institute packed in nine large crates. Since this time the Collection has retained its original character and has been expanded through donations, gifts and purchases.

The estates of the theatre administrator Othmar Keindl (1877-?), the actor Josef Nesper and the opera singer Ludwig Wullner (1858-1938) as well as the archives of the Urania Private Theatre Society (Urania Privattheatergesellschaft) and the Hainto Seitler Circus have all been incorporated into the Collection.

Library of the Theater Institute of the Free University
(Theaterwissenschaftliches Institut der FU)
Riemeisterstr. 21-23, 1000 Berlin 37

The development of the library of the Theater Institute and the Institute itself is largely due to the efforts of Professor Dr. Hans Knudsen (1886-1971). Knudsen had succeeded Max Herrmann (1865-1942), the founder of the Theater Institute of the Friedrich Wilhelm University (the present day Humboldt University in East Berlin), as head of this Institute. Immediately following the war, Knudsen located several of his former students and commenced holding lectures and seminars in a partially bomb-damaged building of the former Kaiser Wilhelm Society (Kaiser-Wilhelm-Gesellschaft) in The Thielallee in Dahlem where the Americans had stored the library of Dr. Hans Lebedes, who had committed suicide. Since the library of the Theater Institute had been partially destroyed in the bombings and the extant part had been evacuated from Berlin, this library, later purchased from Lebedes' relatives, was most welcome.

At the same time, Knudsen tried to save the holdings of the former Society for Theater History from the rising ground water in the basement of the Prussian State Bank, where they had been stored. With several of his students, Knudsen brought the bulk of the books out of the basement and carted them with hand-drawn carts and in briefcases to the building in The Thielallee. The library was further increased by a donation from the author Friedrich Michael, which was transported out of the East sectors by the students.

In 1948, the library of Julius Petersen was placed on permanent loan in the Theater Institute. It consisted of 500 volumes with its own catalogue and has been kept intact. Today, a student supervises this library on the second floor of the Institute.

In 1950, the manuscript and picture collection of the old Berlin merchant Carl Heinrich Gerold was purchased. Consisting of autographs and hand-colored role pictures from 1780 to 1870, it had been found in a trunk which had miraculously survived the war. With the approval of the publishers, Knudsen was able to donate to the Institute library the stage plays he received for review purposes for the "Dramaturgische Blätter," a periodical which he edited. It formed the nucleus of a library of modern plays.

Since the founding of the Free University, the remaining holdings of the reestablished Society for Theater History had been housed with the library of the Theater Institute. In May, 1953, they were presented to the Institute by the Society.

While Eberhard Marx was working on his dissertation "Friedrich Wilhelm Gubitz and the Revival of German Woodcarving in the 19th Century," he discovered that Gubitz's granddaughter had inherited the estate of this Berlin woodworker and sometime theatre critic. Gubitz (1786-1870) had married the youngest daughter of the great hero actor of the Berlin National Theater, Johann Friedrich Ferdinand Fleck (1757-1801). In 1843, Gubitz had tried to obtain Fleck's letters from his mother-in-law, Luise Schrock, for Karl August Varnhagen von Ense's manuscript collection. Following her death, Gubitz obtained the letters from Fleck's estate in 1846. The Gubitz estate also contained letters and contracts of other famous actors from the period from 1787 to 1870. Gubitz's granddaughter, Mrs. Erika Schwarz, gave Knudsen this estate for the Theater Institute in the fall of 1953.

The Union of German Stage Members (Genossenschaft Deutscher Buhenangehorige) gave theatre and promptbooks and playbills from the estate of the actor and Regisseur Paul Petersz (1891-1945). In December, 1954, the relatives of Else Moest, the wife of the actor and Regisseur Friedrich Moest (1866-1948); the actress Mara Feldern-Forster (1870-1951); and the Berlin theatre director and actor Achim von Biel (1900-1954) all presented their collections to the Institute.

In the spring of 1955, Dr. Constantin Constant of the Institute of the former Friedrich Wilhelm University in Vienna, gave the Institute his entire library of plays and film literature. At the same time, the Berlin-Steglitz Public Library gave the Institute approximately 300 volumes of early theatre books and plays. Later, the estate of the scene designer Traugott Muller (1895-1944) was obtained by the Institute.

In the fall of 1972, the Institute moved to Riemeister Strasse 21-23. The library is on the ground floor and the Unruh Collection is in the basement. Since the fall of 1974, a trained librarian runs the library. Theatre students supervise the special sections of the library: the Peterson Collection, the slide collection, the newspaper clipping collection of Berlin and German theatre reviews and the video collection.

Art Library
(Kunstbibiliothek)
Jebensstr. 2, 1000 Berlin 12

The present Art Library was originally part of the Arts and Crafts Museum (Kunstgewerbemuseum), which was founded in 1867. Since this museum was originally planned as an institution for the education of future artists, the library attached to it was divided into three sections which have remained up to the present: the academic art library, the graphic collection and the Lipperheide Costume Library. The graphic and costume libraries have holdings which are of special interest to theatre researchers.

The fame of the graphic collection is based primarily on the ornamental engraving collection, begun in 1886 with the purchase of the Destailleur Paris Collection, and the freehand drawing collection. Later, the Pacetti and the Marc Rosenberg collections were added. These collections contain scene designs for about 400 productions from the seventeenth to the nineteenth centuries. A collection of posters, programs, fly sheets and promotional brochures of the theatre since 1945 also forms part of the theatre holdings.

The world-famous, unique Lipperheide Costume Library is the result of the collecting activities of the fashion publisher Franz von Lipperheide (1838-1906), who collected books, graphics and paintings on and related to the history of dress.

Prior to 1870, the field of costume had scarcely been researched.

In that year, Lipperheide began to gather all relevant material for his library and to catalogue the obscure and scattered sources of this discipline. He included the fundamental original works as well as the important secondary literature and the illustrative works of his century. Within thirty years, he had assembled almost everything which related to this subject.

When it became clear to Lipperheide that such a collection should be made accessible, he opened it to the public beginning in 1896. Since then, it has been utilized by many theatre costume and scene designers for information for their designs. To insure that this library would not be broken up following his death, Lipperheide gave it to the Prussian State in 1899 with the wish that it remain intact and be named after him. The approximately 5500 books, a large number of separate sheets arranged systematically by country and subject, about 2700 freehand drawings, 23,700 sheets of reproductions, about 2500 photos and 686 paintings and 200 minatures were turned over to the Arts and Crafts Museum.

The curators of the Lipperheide Library continue to expand it with the purchase of new as well as old publications. Materials relating to theatre and film were significant additions. In 1905, the holdings were published in a book catalogue, which became a collector's item after it went out of print. In 1965, a new catalogue was published for the centenary of the Library, in which the new acquisitions as well as the original holdings were listed. The books are listed chronologically by year of publication within subject groupings and the catalogue has an author and a subject index.

The losses caused by World War II amounted to about ten percent of the holdings, with most occurring in the costume design collection. Few of the paintings have been retained in the present library. The bulk of them is to be found on the Museum Island in East Berlin in the Art Gallery (Gemalde Gallerie) of the State Museums of Berlin, where they have been stored following their cleaning.

Today, the holdings of the Library have been increased by one third over those of 1905 and consist of more than 12,000 books and 30,000 sheets of graphics. Many theatre costume designs, primarily in the form of individual sheets, are to be found in the Library.

Archives of the Academy of Arts
(Akademie der Künste)
Hanseatenweg 10, 1000 Berlin 21

The archive of the Academy of Arts is a successor to the archive of the Prussian Academy of Arts (Preussische Akademie der Künste) in Berlin, which was founded in 1696 by the Kurfurst Friedrich III and his wife, Sophie Charlotte. During its history, it was moved from time to time, especially during the Nazi years, when the Academy itself ceased to exist. In 1954, the Academy was reestablished in the West, and in 1960, it moved with its archive into a new building which was designed by Werner Duttmann and which was financed by the German-American industrialist Henry H. Reichwald, a Berliner by birth.

The core of the archive, which like the Academy itself is divided into six units: visual arts, architecture, music, literature, performing arts and the general collections and archives, is called the Archive of the Prussian Academy of Arts. It contains approximately 400,000 original documents and artistic objects from the Prussian Academy from 1696 to 1945.

The present head of the archive, Professor Dr. Walter Huder, is primarily responsible for the developments which have occurred since 1956. When a student at the Free University, he had problems finding a copy of Georg Kaiser's play, *Die Bürger von Calais*, since the Nazis had removed all of Kaiser's works from the libraries. It became Huder's wish to publish a critical edition of Kaiser's works, but no publisher was willing to invest in the project unless a sponsor could be found. In 1956, during a walk in the Musausstrasse in Dahlem, Huder saw the sign of the newly-founded Academy of Arts, of which Kaiser was a former member. He went in and convinced the Academy that such a project was worthy of its support. Negotiations were begun with Kaiser's widow and on October 5, 1956, Kaiser's estate was obtained by the Academy.

During these negotiations, it was agreed that Huder would become the head of the projected Georg Kaiser Archive. Shortly thereafter, Huder submitted his plan for the further development of the Georg Kaiser Archive to the Academy. It was to be built up by collecting "manuscripts and the printed primary and secondary literature, which should be obtained without cost if possible by appealing to the mentality and the social situation of the persons possessing the material in order to conserve the allocated budget of the archive for the realization of an edition of the dramas." This was a method to which Huder would resort often in the future years so that he could expand the Georg Kaiser Archive and acquire other archives and collections on an acquisition budget of only $750 (today $1500)!

On March 15, 1957, the Georg Kaiser Archive was officially opened and marked the beginning of a development which would make the archives the most important literary archive in Germany next to the Schiller National Museum in Marbach.

Even at this early stage, Huder planned to develop it into an archive for all the writers in the Academy through the acquisition of the estates of the former members of the literature section as had been accomplished with the Kaiser estate. Today not only has this aim been largely realized but goes much beyond the original scope. Now there are archive divisions for all five of the Academy sections.

The Hegelian principle that truth can only be found in the entirety has been applied to the development of the individual archives. The staff tries to augment the estates with additional primary materials as well as the secondary literature and newspaper articles. The goal is not only the concentration and accumulation of cultural wares, but above all the stimulation of activities for continuing research and evaluation by making them accessible. The public is to be made aware of the holdings through the following activities:

1. Exhibitions. Every archive and collection is opened with an exhibition after the necessary cataloguing of the material is completed. An "archive" is used in the sense of an entire estate and a "collection" refers to a partial estate or material collected on a specific subject. These exhibitions are planned so that they can be sent to other cities and are accompanied by a catalogue with lesser-known photographs, essays by prominent researchers and a bibliography. In addition, conferences with well-known authorities from all over the world are organized which results in a publication of the lectures and the most important sections of the discussions.

2. Supervising research. Over 700 projects have been realized using the resources of the archives.

3. Help in the edition of the complete critical editions. Editions

of the works of authors, artists and architects whose estates are administered by the Archive are encouraged and augmented with previously unpublished material.

4. Collective dramaturgy. A special activity of the archives is what Huder calls "collective dramaturgy." Copies of reviews, programs, scene photos and even posters of former productions of the drama are sent upon request to theatres or TV stations so that they can be used for the new staging. In return, they send the material from their production to the archive and are thus indirect participants in the next staging.

5. Establishing sister archives. In order to encourage research abroad, photocopies of the holdings of the archive are kept in sister archives abroad, which insures that the material will not be lost. Up to now, the following sister archives have been established: the Georg Kaiser Archive at the University of Texas in Austin and the University of Alberta in Edmonton, Canada; the Ödön von Horváth Archive at the University of Wisconsin in Madison and the University of Stockholm; and the Alfred Kerr Archive at Yale Unviersity.

The archives and collections in the Academy of Arts has focused on artists who were active in Berlin during the twenties. An extension to this is the Theater in Exile Collection, which documents the German speaking theatre during the years the Fascists were in power and which provides much material explaining the contemporary theatre development in many of the countries where the exiles worked. The following archives of theatre-relevant artists are in the Academy:

Visual Art Section: George Grosz (1893-1959).

Architecture Section: Hugo Haring (1882-1958).

Literature Section: Maximilian Böttcher (1872-1950), Arnolt Bronnen (1885-1940), Farieluise Fleisser (1901-1974), Wolfgang Goetz (1885-1955), Ödön von Horváth (1901-1938), Georg Kaiser (1878-1945), Walter Meckauer (1889-1966), Walter von Molo (1880-1958), Gerhart Pohl (1902-1966).

Performing Arts Section: Julius Bab (1880-1955), Ludwig Berger (1892-1969), Ernst Deutsch (1890-1969), Käthe Dorsch (1890-1957), Tilla Durieux (1880-1971), Alexander Engel (1869-19?), Jurgen Fehling (1885-1968), Alexander Granach (1890-1945), Julius Hart (1859-1930), Heinz Hilpert (1890-1967), Alfred Kerr (1867-1948), Fritz Kortner (1892-1970), Leonard Steckel (1901-

1971), Heinz Tietien (1881-1967), Elsa Wagner (1881-1975), Mary Wigman (1886-1973).

Alongside these archives are the following theatre-relevant collections:

Music Section: Alfred Einstein (1880-1924).

Literature Section: Lion Feuchtwanger (1884-1958), Leonard Frank (1882-1961), Paul Gurk (1880-1953), Carl Hauptmann (1858-1921), Arno Holz (1863-1929), Paul Kornfeld (1889-1942?), Alfred Neumann (1895-1952), Ernst Toller (1893-1939).

Performing Arts Section: Roma Bahn (1896-1975), Elow (Berlin cabaret from 1926 to 1933), Florian Kienzl (1894-1972), Max Reinhardt (1873-1943), Rotraut Richter (1915-1947), Theater in Exile, "Thema" (the emigrant publishing house), Paul Wegener (1894-1948).

(Not all of the above have been completely catalogued because of the limited staff and budget.)

A good example of how the work of the archives can reach the public can be seen in the revival of Ödön von Horváth, who had been largely forgotten at the end of World War II. The opening of the Horváth Archive led to a major reevaluation of his work and today, Horváth's works are regularly presented on the German stage and television. Many of his plays have also been translated and performed in other countries. As a result of the archive's activities, he has emerged as one of the major German dramatists.

There are several other collections which bear mentioning:

The Press Archive contains newspaper clippings going back to 1826. In 1957 it was organized and expanded into its present form. It contains press material from Germany and abroad on the former and present members of the Academy, on artists not in the Academy, on activities of the institution, on events and general themes on the entire art world, on art prizes and on other academies. Of special interest is the considerable amount of press material on the history of the Berlin Kroll Opera. In all, the Press Archive has about 850,000 archive sheets which are catalogued and arranged systematically in folders.

On July 8, 1970, the Archive was able to obtain a major part of the Ludwig Berger Shakespearean Library, one of the largest such collections, when it was placed on auction in Cologne. Funds were provided for this purpose from the German Lottery.

Another of the Archive collections is the Walter von Molo Library, which contains one of the largest collections of Nazi literature. Since the literature of this period was almost completely removed from German libraries after 1945, the Molo Library is invaluable for research of this period.

The Wilhelm Richter Theater Collection is the work of a passionate Berlin theatre-goer. Wilhelm Richter attended almost every theatre premiere in Berlin from 1906 to his death in 1961 and carefully collected all the programs of the productions as well as all the reviews which appeared in the press. In addition, he preserved almost all of the Festschriften of the Berlin stages, numerous drama and opera texts, almost the complete volumes of literary and dramaturgical periodicals of this period, scene designs, playbills, pamphlets and material on film premieres. Up to 1928, the reviews were carefully arranged and bound. The later reviews have been arranged chronologically in folders and the entire Collection has been catalogued. A smaller but similar collection of programs and reviews belonging to theatre critic Dr. Erich Krafft has been added to the Richter Collection. The period after 1961 has been maintained so that an almost complete newspaper clipping archive of the Berlin theatre and film since 1906 is readily available.

Archive of the Land Berlin
(Landesarchiv)
Kalckreuthstr. 1/2, 1000 Berlin 30

The Landesarchiv, which received this name in 1951 as a result of the Berlin constitutional change in 1950, tries to present a total documentation of the history of Berlin. The older holdings had been either stored in the western sector of the city at the end of the war or they were acquired by purchase or as gifts. The archive possesses no written documents from the Berlin Magistrate Administration prior to 1945.

The legal predecessor of the Landesarchiv was the former City Archive of the City of Berlin (Stadtarchiv der Stadt Berlin), which dates from 1307 and beyond. Prior to World War II, during which it suffered major losses, it was housed in the Berlin Rathaus. The division of Berlin in November, 1948, also resulted in a division of the archive. On December 1, 1948, the work of the present Landes-archiv began almost without archival material in the "Hotel am Zoo" on the Kurfurstendamm. In the following years, it changed quarters several times. The move to its present location was completed in 1976.

Since much primary material on the Berlin theatre was either destroyed in the war and its aftermath or is difficult to obtain because of the division of the city, the Berlin newspaper collection in the Landesarchiv is invaluable. This collection, though incomplete, is continually being expanded and has either microfilm or bound copies of most of the Berlin newspapers going back to the eighteenth century.

Equally valuable is the collection of about 14,000 playscripts which were submitted to the Berlin theatre censors. During the war, the attic of the Police Headquarters was cleared out and the entire files of the former Censor Division of the police were unearthed here. (Although theatre censorship was terminated in Prussia in 1848, it was revived in Berlin in 1851 and continued until the end of the monarchy in 1918.) The plays, which were later transferred to the Landesarchiv, and the censor files, which were later destroyed, were taken to the Prussian Secret State Archive (Preussische Geheime Staatsarchiv). The titles are listed in a book catalogue along with those police files relating to the Berlin theatre of the nineteenth century in the Landesarchiv. A listing of the locations of the theatre and places of performance in Berlin is appended to the catalogue.

Since 1970, the Landesarchiv has been further enriched by the acquisition of the Matthes Theater Historical Collection, the Koerner Theater Historical Collection and the Günter Neumann Library.

In 1912, Eugen B. Matthes, a publisher and administrator, had received hand-written role books, pictures and autographed letters of famous actors as a birthday present on his fifteenth birthday from his actor-father. The gift became the basis of his collection, which he called the "Archive for Theater History." Throughout his life, he added to it playbills, programs, posters, newspaper clippings, auto-graphs, pictures, medals, sculptures and recordings with a special section devoted to Max Reinhardt. The entire collection was housed in his Wilmersdorf apartment, Spessartstrasse 4, and could be used by anyone interested in it. On April 9, 1970, Matthes sold it to the Landesarchiv, which used lottery money to pay for it, and it was renamed the Matthes Theater Historical Collection. It has been kept intact within the Landesarchiv.

Rolf Koerner, a civil service administrator, was a theatre enthusiast who collected between 1942 and 1972 such material on the theatre as programs, tickets, newspaper clippings and pictures all relating to the Berlin theatre, opera, dance and concert life. A special section consists of newspaper clippings, pictures and programs on the actor Werner Krauss (1884-1954) between 1926 and 1969. On December 18, 1973, Koerner's widow, Hildegard Koerner, gave the collection to the Landesarchiv with the wish that it remain intact and be called the Koerner Theater Historical Collection.

On December 17, 1974, the Landesarchiv bought the library of Günter Neumann (1913-1952), the well-known Berlin cabaret performer. It contains, among other things, Neumann's music, manuscripts and the magazine *Insulaner*, which Neumann edited.

Although the institutions which have been described thus far are those of primary interest for theatre research in West Berlin, there are several others which have special holdings either directly or indirectly relevant to theater research. They are:

Working Group for Meeting Buildings of the Technical University
(Arbeitsgruppe für Versammlungsbauten der TU)
Strasse des 17. Juni Nr. 150/152, 1000 Berlin 12

The Working Group for Meeting Buildings, formerly the Institute for Theater Buildings (Institut für Theaterbau), was established after the war to serve as a consultation center for all questions relating to theatre construction and technology. Its library contains literature on theatre architecture and technology. In addition, there are building plans, a card catalogue, correspondence and construction material from various sources. This is augmented by periodicals and slides, which are in part from the partial estate of Thomas Munter, the founder of the Institute.

Ludwig Geiger Library
(Ludwig-Geiger-Bibliothek)
Stadtbücherei Wilmersdorf
Brandenburgische Str. 2, 1000 Berlin 31

The Ludwig Geiger Library is housed in the Berlin-Wilmersdorf

Public Library. Geiger (1848-1919) was a Goethe specialist and secondary literature on Goethe forms the bulk of the Library. Geiger was also very interested in the theatre, and between 1902 and 1919, he was head of the Society for Theater History, which he had helped found. Since the majority of the books are from the nineteenth century and many of them are difficult to find elsewhere, this little-known library is invaluable for theatre research.

America Memorial Library
(Amerika-Gedenkbibliothek)
Blucherplatz 2, 1000 Berlin 61

The America Memorial Library, the central public library in West Berlin, has three partial archives bearing on the theatre: those of the theatre critic Theodor Fontane (1819-1898), and the playwrights Arno Holz and Johannes Schlaf (1862-1941). In addition there is a Heinrich von Kleist Collection containing a nearly complete collection of Kleist (1777-1811) editions in almost every language as well as extensive secondary literature on Kleist. In 1976, the Society for Theater Research gave its recently acquired bibliographic collection to the Library. It contains predominantly literature from Eastern European countries which the Society obtained as exchange publications. This literature has not yet been catalogued.

State Library
(Staatsbibliothek)
Potsdamer Str. 53, 1000 Berlin 30

Included with its large holdings of theatre literature, the State Library has the estates of the following theatre-related people: the dramatists Gerhart Hauptmann (1862-1946), Gustav Freytag (1816-1895), Gotthold Ephraim Lessing (1729-1781), Jakob Michael Reinhold Lenz (1751-1792), Arno Holz, Ludwig Tieck (1773-1853), Gerhart Pohl, the actors Konrad Dietrich Ekhof (1720-1778), Jakob Tiedtke (1875-1960), Lina Fuhr (1828-1906), the theatre journalist Alfred Holzbock, the opera composer Arnold Schönberg and the theatre critics Walther Karsch (1906-1975) and Theodor Fontane. It also possesses the Lessing Theater Prompt Book Collection.

Since the end of World War II, the theatre resources in West Berlin have made enormous strides under many hardships. One very major problem remains the lack of a central institution for the coordination of the acquisition of theatre research material. Consequently, the institutions compete with each other for the material (for example, the Academy of Arts, the America Memorial Library and the State Library all have Arno Holz collections), thereby driving the prices up higher than is necessary. Equally bothersome is the limited financing and the lack of adequate staffing to catalogue, supervise and administer the material which is available. Nonetheless, the staffs are generally very helpful and they do their best to make research as fruitful as possible.

THE UNIVERSITY OF BRISTOL THEATRE COLLECTION

by George Rowell

In its early years the Drama Department of Bristol University was twice the recipient of generous grants from the Rockefeller Foundation. These grants were used for a number of purposes: the conversion and equipment of a Drama Studio, a series of lectures by distinguished theatre practitioners, and the purchase of materials which formed the nucleus of the Theatre Collection.

These materials were originally housed in the University Library, and were consequently chosen to fill gaps in the Library's holdings. Priority was given to records of staging methods, including such comprehensive works as *Monumenta Scenica*, editions of Serlio and Sabbattini, and Gordon Craig's *"The Pretenders": A Production*. From the start, however, the Collection was not limited to published material. Manuscript items associated with the Anglo-American actor Herman Vezin were an early acquisition, and such exhibition features as William Etty's portrait of Charles Kean as Lear and eleven of the silver "tickets" issued in 1766 to the original proprietors of the Theatre Royal, Bristol, were purchased from these funds.

With its move in 1960 to a home of its own, the Collection was able to widen its scope and increase its holdings. The acquisition of playbills from all periods was stepped up, inspired by the gift from Mr. Charles Landstone of a comprehensive run of London first-night programmes from 1945 to 1957. Mr. Landstone was also responsible for persuading the Bristol Old Vic to donate their records, though these are only available for examination after a lapse of seven years. About this time, the Arts Council placed on indefinite loan their collection of original designs for the Company's early productions, and further items of local interest were acquired, including a series of costume designs for Bristol pantomimes in the 1880s and 1890s by the celebrated Victorian designer Wilhelm (John Charles Pitcher).

The biggest stimulus of the 1960s was, however, the purchase of

---

George R. Rowell is Professor of Drama at the University of Bristol and a noted Victorian theatre scholar.

the Richard Southern accession. Dr. Southern's interest in theatre architecture and stage machinery had resulted in the accumulation of a remarkable collection of graphic material in this field, predominantly but by no means exclusively British, and extending into such unexpected areas as the London County Council's records of West End theatre buildings in 1936. This material has been widely drawn on for teaching purposes and for book illustration, both by members of the Department and other writers.

Although there was no original material amongst the graphic items, the accession did include twelve unpublished volumes on British scenic artists, compiled by the pioneer theatre historian, W.J. Lawrence, and presented by him to Richard Southern. A high proportion of the books included in this accession had also belonged originally to Lawrence, and many are annotated by him. Amongst the most widely travelled items acquired in this accession are the three large-scale models of an Elizabethan theatre, Wren's Drury Lane, and the Georgian Playhouse, Richmond, Yorkshire, made to Dr. Southern's designs. These have been frequently exhibited, and invariably prove a source of debate and delight.

When the Drama Department took over its present building in 1967, arrangements were made for the Theatre Collection to be housed under the same roof as the teaching rooms and studio theatre. For the first time the Collection could offer suitable accommodation for study, and the new premises provided stack-rooms, exhibition space and audio-visual facilities. The present Keeper, Ann Brooke Barnett, and her Assistant, Christopher Robinson, have thus been able to build up and catalogue the Collection as befits its importance and interest. Not all the accessions have been books or prints; two impressive pictures placed on indefinite loan by the Vic-Wells Association are Samuel Drummond's well-known portrait of Edmund Kean as Richard III (1814) and Somerled Macdonald's portrait of Matheson Lang as Hamlet.

In 1973 the University was able to purchase from the family of Sir Herbert Beerbohm Tree a substantial collection of material relating to his tenure of the Haymarket and Her Majesty's Theatres. Virtually every play Tree staged at these theatres is represented in some form; there are, for example, promptbooks for seventy-four of his productions, in many cases several such books, recording revivals and touring versions. (A complete list follows this essay.) There are original designs by artists such as Percy Macquoid, Percy Anderson, "Karl," and Byam Shaw, and extensive photographic coverage of Tree's later productions. Amongst the promptbooks, those for Tree's spectacular Shakespeare productions are especially valuable, while amongst more modern plays, that for *Pygmalion* is undoubtedly the most important. Most of the promptbooks are supplemented by various "plots" (lighting, property, even "shoe" and "murmur" plots), and some of the music originally used has survived.

Another musical item in the Collection is the full, cued-in score for Martin-Harvey's production of *The Corsican Brothers* (by the unhappily named Von Franckenstein), a rare example of this most ephemeral form of theatrical record. In the Tree Collection there is also a monumental series of sixty-four volumes of press cuttings, covering thirty years of Tree's career, and a fascinating assortment of account books recording the fortunes of his theatre from the turn of the century. The only correspondence is a bound volume of letters of congratulation on Tree's knighthood in 1909.

The light which the Tree Collection throws on theatre history at the end of Victoria's reign and throughout Edward VII's has fostered further acquisition of material from this period, notably a complete run of the periodical *The Theatre* (1878-97), and a nearly complete set of *Who's Who in the Theatre* (from 1912) and its predecessor *The Green Room Book* (1906-1909). The Collection has also branched out into areas hitherto little represented, for example classical and oriental theatre, and is now building up its holding on the history of the cinema. It aims to cover the contemporary theatre, and to carry a wide-ranging selection of relevant periodicals.

The University of Bristol Theatre Collection is primarily a teaching-aid for its students, both undergraduate and postgraduate. Located as it is, not only in a University but in a city of theatrical importance, both past and present, it also draws scholars and practitioners of the theatre from far beyond the academic body, as the Visitors' Book testifies. While its resources offer no prospect of developing on the scale of some of the great European or North American collections, it gives every indication of achieving an importance scarcely contemplated at its inception, even by the far-seeing benefactors of the Rockefeller Foundation.

BEERBOHM TREE SCRIPT COLLECTION

Admirable Bashville: 2 scripts; 3 parts
Admiral Guinea: 3 prompt copies and 2 books for parts
Agatha: 14 copies; reviews, etc.
An African Millionaire: 1 script
Antony and Cleopatra: plots (lights, costumes, etc.) ; reviews
Ariadne auf Naxos: reviews; 2 prompt copies
Ballad Monger: prompt copy; reviews
Barabbas: 1 script
Beau Austin: 2 prompt copies; parts; reviews
Beethoven: prompt copy; 2 scripts; parts; reviews
Beloved Vagabond: reviews; prompt copy; parts; photos
Blue Lagoon: script
Bunch of Violets: plots; 5 prompt copies; parts; reviews
Business is Business: portraits; prompt copy; parts; reviews
Caesar's Wife: prompt copy; parts; scripts
Captain Swift: 2 prompt copies; parts; plots; copies; reviews
Carnac Sahib: 4 prompt copies; reviews
Charlatan: 3 prompt copies; ms; reviews
Colonel Newcombe: 5 prompt copies; parts; plots; photos; 2
    portraits; reviews
Comedy and Tragedy: 6 copies
Compromising Case: prompt copy
Critic: 1 script; plot
Dancing Girl: prompt copy, parts, 6 copies; plots; reviews
Dangerfield: script
Darling of the Gods: prompt copy; scripts; parts; plots; photos;
    reviews; souvenir
David Copperfield: prompt copy; scripts; parts; photos; reviews
Door Upon the Latch: script
Drake: 2 prompt copies; parts; plots; reviews; photos
Duchess of Bayswater; prompt copy; photos; reviews
Emily: script
Enemy of the People: plots; 3 prompt copies; reviews
Eternal City: script; 2 prompt copies; copies; parts; reviews
False Gods: scripts; parts; photos; souvenirs; reviews; 2 prompt
    copies

Faust: prompt copy; plots; script; photos; reviews
Fedora: plots; 2 prompt copies; reviews
Fireside Hamlet: ms
First Night: 2 prompt copies; scripts; parts
Flodden Field: 3 scripts; parts; reviews
Forest of Wild Thyme: script
Fortune's Fool: script
Friend: script
Gordian Knot: reviews; script
Governor of Kentucky: script
Hamlet: photos; 2 prompt copies; parts; reviews
Hannele: 3 prompt copies; plots; copies
Hansel and Gretel: plans; photos
Happy Island: prompt copy; scripts; parts; photos
Heard at the Telephone: scripts
Henry IV: photos; reviews; 3 prompt copies; plots
Henry VIII: photos; 3 prompt copies; plots; reviews; costume
    designs
Herod: copies; plots; souvenir; photos; reviews
His Last Legs: copies
Honour of the Home: script
House of Bondage: scripts; parts; plots
Hypatia: 2 prompt copies; music; copies; parts; souvenir;
    reviews
Incognito: prompt copy; parts; reviews
Intruder: reviews
John a Dreams: prompt copy; parts; scripts; reviews; plots
Joseph and His Brethren: prompt copy; script; photos; reviews
Julius Caesar: souvenir; photos; reviews; music;
    3 prompt copies
Julius Caesar Forum Scene: prompt copy; plots; photos
Katherine and Petruchio: reviews; prompt copy; parts
King John: scripts; plots; 3 prompt copies; reviews
Last of the Dandies: scripts; parts; plots; costume designs;
    reviews
Lethal Hotel: scripts
Macaire: reviews (see also: Robert Macaire)
Macbeth: photos; 2 prompt copies; plots; reviews

Man's Shadow: parts; music; 2 prompt copies; "murmurs" plot;
    prompt copy; reviews
Man Who Was: reviews; scripts; photos
Marie Odile: photos; prompt copy; plots; reviews
Masks and Faces: parts; prompt copy; reviews
Masque of Peace and War; script
Mavourneen; photos
Merchant of Venice: photos; costume designs; "shoe plot," etc. ;
    scenic designs; 2 prompt copies; reviews
Merry Wives of Windsor: photos; costume designs; scripts;
    parts; plots; reviews; prompt copy
Midsummer Night's Dream: souvenirs; costume designs;
    reviews; scripts
Modern Eve: prompt copy
Monsieur Beaucaire: reviews
Much Ado About Nothing: costume designs; reviews; photos;
    plots; 2 prompt copies; scripts
Musketeers: scripts; photos; 2 prompt copies; reviews; costume
    designs
Mystery of Edwin Drood: 3 prompt copies; parts; plots
Nero: souvenirs; portraits; photos; prompt copy; parts;
    costume designs; reviews
O'Flynn: prompt copy; scripts; plots; parts; photos; reviews
Oliver Twist: 2 prompt copies; parts; plots; scripts; many
    photos; souvenirs; programmes; reviews
Once Upon a Time: scripts; reviews; 2 prompt copies
Orpheus in the Underworld: scripts; scene sketches; parts;
    plots; photos; reviews
Othello: photo; 2 prompt copies; scripts; plots; reviews
Partners: prompt copy; parts; reviews
Perfect Gentleman: prompt copy; parts
Peril: 2 prompt copies; photos; reviews
Pinkie and the Fairies: scripts; parts; photos; reviews
Pompadour: 3 prompt copies; reviews
Prince of India: photos
Pygmalion: prompt copy; part; articles
Question of Conscience: script
Ragged Robin: reviews; script; plots; 2 prompt copies

Red Lamp: 3 prompt copies; parts; music; reviews
Resurrection: scripts; 4 prompt copies; parts; plots; reviews
Richard II: reviews; portrait; scripts; photos; prompt copy
Right to Kill: photos; prompt copy; parts; plots
Rip Van Winkle: 3 prompt copies; photos; reviews
Romeo and Juliet: scripts
Russian Tragedy: scripts
Robert Macaire: script
School for Scandal: script; reviews
Seats of the Mighty: 2 prompt copies; parts; reviews
Silver Key: 2 prompt copies; plots; reviews
Silver King: reviews; photo
Six and Eightpence: script
Six Persons: 2 prompt copies; parts; reviews
Step-sisters: script
Tempest: review; 2 prompt copies; photos; souvenir
Tempter: 3 prompt copies; script; parts; music; costume
    designs; reviews
Tilda's New Hat: prompt copy; parts
To Be Sold: script
Trilby: 4 prompt copies; parts; plots; photos; souvenirs;
    programmes; reviews
Twelfth Night: souvenir; 4 prompt copies; reviews; plots; photo
Typhoon: script
Ulysses: scripts; plots; photos; reviews
Ultimatum: scripts
Van Dyck: reviews; prompt copy; scripts
Village Priest: prompt copy; parts; reviews; plots
Vision of Delight: script
Waif: 2 prompt copies; parts
War God: reviews; scripts; parts; plots
Wealth: prompt copy; parts
Winter's Tale: scripts; plots; reviews; photos
Woman of No Importance: 2 prompt copies; parts; reviews

A DOCUMENTARY SYSTEM FOR TELEVISION ARCHIVES

by Gabriele Melischek and Wolfgang Ramjoué

Once upon a time, there was a hopeful young man who was given the order to pile up tin boxes and to file every box in the "big book." And he did that very carefully.

But one day a ne'er-do-well teased the hopeful young man and asked, "Do you know what's in those boxes?" That's when the hopeful young man invented description-cards, but he was annoyed with the nosy questioner and he designed the cards in a way so nobody would know about it except himself. And when more and more boxes were piled up and more and more cards were written, he was given a little tin chest and a hopeful young girl to help him write the cards and put them into the chest.

Many years passed and the hopeful young man wasn't young or hopeful anymore. One day his superiors said, "This man is not qualified for his job. In all those years he has not been able to keep a decent file." The desperate man pointed to the cards in his chest and cried, "My lords, how can I manage that all by myself?" And his superiors took counsel and spoke thus, "He is right. We will give him assistants and that will solve the problem." And the man let his assistants into the secrets of tin boxes and cards and invented tasks for them. Soon he was acknowledged as superior, because he knew better than anybody else how to find something. And there was praise for those assistants who had a very good memory. And they built up a state within the state and called it "archive" and behaved mystically, because they did not want anybody to know that they had no constitution. And they lived happily ever after. . . .

You think this is a bad story? Unfortunately yes, but it is true, because no archive was organized rationally from the beginning. Every insider will certify that all files which have grown gradually have very little system and that many a time very old material can be

Both Dr. Melischek and Ramjoué were formerly associated with ORF (Austrian Radio and Television).

found again only by excellent memory and/or good luck.

In the meantime the first archive generation starting with the beginning of television is near retirement and young employees just don't have the knowledge of the historical events in its earliest years.

The film with the number "one" in the archives of the ORF dates from the year 1957. It is a film about current events similar to any other television company's in the world: there are fashion-shows, fires and disasters and political events. In the first years of television, people were actually happy to be able to produce and broadcast programs and did not spend thought on re-using this very material for the future.

Nowadays we have two problems: 1) either to work up material for retrieval or simply abandon it for good. (The latter course is impossible with the current interest in nostalgia.) Or 2) to make the huge amount of incoming material ready for instant retrieval.

When you learn that Austrian Television stores over half a million films and video-tapes between 20 seconds and four hours long, you can imagine that the information stored within them cannot be handled by "big books" or even card-files anymore.

Television archives are neither libraries nor museums. They perform a service. Our interpretation of the main purpose of an archive is to select and prepare film and tape for re-use in other programs and films. The more accurately every meter of film is analyzed, the higher the yield of the film-stock. Every newly shot and broadcasted minute costs about fifty times more than an "archive minute," which makes this a most important economical item for any television company, which has broadcast so many documentary, semi-documentary and scientific programs like the ORF.

It is obvious that a television archive basically works like any other archive, but in one important respect it has to work in a completely different way. The importance of the film sequence is paramount. Parts of films, produced years ago, can be used to illustrate completely different items in another context. This can be easily demonstrated: watch a documentary film without the soundtrack and you will notice that you could put different narrations under the film.

The analysis of archived film sequence thus provides a readily available supply of background shots, informative material and historical data. Any newspaper archive will contain, for instance, features about the Suez Canal, but a television archive will offer film sequences and pictures of activities.

Of course, first steps toward raw analysis of film-stock have been done a long time ago in television archives all over the world. This can be spoken of as the "second dimension." The third dimension is a completely new way of thinking. Although it may sound visionary or Orwellian, it embraces a system whereby the film-stock is analyzed to discover all facets of the content which can be duly recorded. The records may be in the form of film-stocks and conventional card files, which conceivably can multiply until they are no longer manageable. ORF has already accumulated one and a half million file cards.

An alternative method "pushes us into the cold arms of EDV" (American equivalent: electronic data processing), which has now been subjected to a two-year period of testing for its effectiveness.

Our first task was to find out which data-elements could be well defined into a format for coding by fixed-scale field. For most elements, numerical codes could be established, such as: for the identification of the document, its color, format (6mm, 8mm, super 8, etc.), physical characteristics (e.g., in the case of film: positive, reverse-original, reverse-duplicate, etc.), as well as its technical type (e.g., in the case of tape: high band, low band, etc.) ; then for the kind of copy with regard to its function (e.g., originals, records, copies, etc.). The time or length, date of production, date of broadcast, the kind of program, the date of entrance, the identification of the producer, and the kind of production could also be assigned code numbers. For titles, alphanumerical fields have been assigned. And for all persons related to the production process, such as, directors, designers, actors, etc., a combined code was chosen: the numerical part representing the name. Finally, the content of the document was left for the field called 'abstract.' Here the archivist was free to summarize the description of the visual sequences as well as the subject matter.

The final data sheet containing all of these elements was developed and tested in cooperation with all the German-language television archives.

Since 1970, a commission called "Regelwerk Fernsehen" has included representatives from all German television stations and since

1971, Austrian and Swiss delegates as well. "Regelwerk" means a complete list of rules, by which you classify, analyze, interpret and describe all data: backgrounds, sequences, themes and subjects of films and video-tapes. The plan has been to set up an EDV-network among Germany, Switzerland and Austria in order to be able to ask for and retrieve any desired material from the archives of member constituents. The three basic conditions for this kind of network were: a common language, German, in this case; the second, a uniform system of analysis for all participant archives; and the third, the desirability to have all informations at once which can be done only by on-line (terminal) system. The first two conditions have been met for the "Regelwerk Fernsehen."

We knew that the "Regelwerk" could not be practicable at once. It was designed for an on-line (terminal) system with direct access for anyone at anytime. Our plan was to store all abstracts without assigned keywords in order to generate a thesaurus through searching a natural language text. In our own case, a number of selected keywords would be reproduced on the conventional file cards while at the same time the complete data could be stored on magnetic tape up to the moment the ORF would decide to take part in the information network among German-language television archives or to build up its information retrieval system independently. Unfortunately, in Austria, EDV belongs to the commercial department of ORF and is used for computerizing staff and production costs only. Nobody wants to spend money on the storage of archive-data which is the basic requirement. The only missing element is a terminal, since additional staff would not have been necessary.

There are other important ramifications of such a system as "Regelwerk." There is a real possibility that it could serve as an instrument for valid scientific and social analyses.

Two recent projects have demonstrated how it may be integrated into scientific and sociological investigations. The first one has been done by Doris Graber at the University of Illinois and has tried to show more appropriate and adequate content analysis techniques for televised political news by developing a complex audio-visual coding scheme. The elements outlined by Doris Graber are the separation of a general theme and supporting episodes; and the identification of cues and cliches for different subject areas. She has searched factors for external and internal situations and she has worked out a concept of noise which permits elimination of non-relevant images. Her approach is still quite experimental and still incomplete in other news areas. But she claims to be far enough along in research and experimentation to realize that accurate coding of the information by televised news is feasible and interpretable.

And even if Doris Graber's claims that audio-visual coding is prohibitively expensive are correct, she also suggested that the price cannot be considered too high for data files on the medium which is now the most universally used source for political news.

The other project has become part of a multi-national study which has tried to show the broad trends in the content of television drama and in the conceptions about social reality of child and adult audiences. This project of television content and effects has been developed by George Gerbner at the Annenberg School of Communications (University of Pennsylvania) and it consists of two main parts: message system analysis and cultivation analysis. The message system analysis is based on annual samples of nationally broadcast dramatic television programs. The object of his analysis, Gerbner points out, is to provide systematic, cumulative, and reliable observations concerning the world of television drama.

Based on a television documentation system developed by Gerbner it may be possible to achieve higher statistical validity through a sophistication of his recording instrument and answer such questions as does viewing cultivate assumptions implicit in the world of television drama? What impact does television drama have on how regular viewers think about facts of life and society? Do these conceptions depend on amount or kind of exposure, on age, sex, ethnic background? And do they change if and when the patterns of dramatic programming change?

Gerbner's systematic observation of our "symbolic environment" becomes imperative for the development of indicators and profiles of cultural trends relevant to scientific purpose and public policy. And to go even further, for cross-cultural comparison, probably the "Regelwerk" ought to be an international one.

This article is based on a paper presented by the authors at the Congress of SIBMAS in Vienna, 1976.

THE INTERNATIONAL THEATRE INSTITUTE

by Elizabeth Burdick

Doing research in a foreign country frequently presents problems that appear insurmountable. The International Theatre Institute lends professional and moral support to the scholar working in a country where difficulties may be caused by differences in method, language, and library requirements.

Seventy centers, affiliates, and associates of the ITI on six continents maintain quarters for the express purpose of rendering assistance, improving understanding, and strengthening the artistic and spiritual alliance among theatre people of all nations. From Moscow to Malaysia, this organization, which was established after a Paris meeting in 1947 at the behest of UNESCO, provides information and offers research assistance to students, teachers, scholars, writers, theatre professionals, or to anyone in need of its services. Each center represents all aspects of its country's theatre and endeavors, in the mandate of the ITI Charter, to "promote the exchange of knowledge and practice in the theatre arts."

Since 1949 when the Charter was accepted by the United States, Rosamond Gilder has been the active president of the ITI/US. In 1968, after twenty years as a department of ANTA, ITI/US became an independent, non-profit service organization, with Martha W. Coigney as its director.

Housed in light, airy offices overlooking Broadway, ITI/US maintains one of the most pleasant libraries for world-wide theatre information in this city. Coffee is served to the visitor while the director of the theatre collection and the staff make every effort to solve the researcher's problems or to prepare him for research outside the United States.

The card catalogue of the collection includes references to theatre in 118 countries. Nearly 5000 foreign plays, representing seventy-one countries, are catalogued, and the American play index

Elizabeth Burdick is Director of the theatre collection in the American Centre of International Theatre Institute in New York.

records 1700 titles. The Centre receives and shelves 185 foreign and domestic periodicals on the performing groups and maintains files documenting the activities of 700 performing groups across the United States. Although nearly 3500 volumes are housed here, the core of the library is non-book material and theatre ephemera. Thousands of newsletters, yearbooks, programs, press releases, production schedules, brochures, reviews, monographs, clippings, and photographs from and about theatre around the world are catalogued annually.

In one year representatives of thirty-eight countries and thirty-five of the United States used the collection. Requests ranged from a director of a theatre school in India who required a bibliography on acting and improvisation to a producer in Denmark who needed Off-Broadway posters for a set design. The library staff edits and publishes *Theatre Notes*, a newsletter on companies touring the United States and abroad. Issued ten times annually, it is distributed free of charge. ITI/US distributes in this country *International Theatre Information*, the bilingual review and information organ of the ITI Secretariat, Paris, and sends *The Drama Review* to the major ITI Centres abroad.

This is only a small segment typifying the varied services rendered by ITI/US. Depending upon the space, staff, and funds, the services of other centers throughout the world vary. A researcher intending overseas travel should contact the United States office to confirm the latest information regarding specific centers and to obtain a correct list of their addresses.

NATIONAL CENTRES OF THE ITI

Argentina
Argentine Centre of the ITI
a.b.s. Argentores
Pacheco de Melo 1820
Buenos Aires
  Pres.: Mr. Edmundo Guibourg
  Sec. Gen.: Mr. Saulo Benavente
  tel.: Mr. Benavente 41 58 86
   (10.30-14h)

Australia
Australian Centre of the ITI
P.O. Box 137
Kings Cross, 2011 N.S.W.
  Pres.: Prof. Robert Quentin
  Sec.: Ms. Marlis Thiersch
  tel.: 357 12 00 (week: 9-17h)

Austria
Austrian Centre of the ITI
Breite Gasse 12
A.1070 Wien
  Pres.: Prof. E. Haüssermann
  Sec.: Ms. Helga Dostal
  tel.: 93 84 67 (week: 10.30-13h)

Belgium
Belgian Centre of the ITI
c/o Mark Hermans
Rudolfstraat 33
B-2000 Antwerpen
  Co-Pres.: Mr. Alfons van Impe
  and Mr. Georges Sion
  Sec.: Mr. Mark Hermans
  tel.: 03/37 38 67

Bulgaria
Bulgarian Centre of the ITI
c/o VITIZ "Kr. Sarafov"
108 rue Rakovsky
Sofia
  Pres.: Prof. Philippe Philippov
  Sec.: Dr. Elisabeth Sotirova

Colombia
Colombian Centre of the ITI
Teatro Experimental de Cali
Calle 7a No. 8-63
Apartado Aereo 2050
Cali
  Mr. Enrique Buenaventura

Cuba
Cuban Centre of the ITI
Av. Kohly No. 151
Esquina 32 Nuevo Vedado
Havana
  Pres.: Mr. René de la Cruz
  Sec.: Mr. Ignacio Gutierrez
  tel.: 3-6894 (week: 8-16.30h)

Czechoslovakia
Czechoslovak Centre of the ITI
rue Celetnà 17
110.01 Prague 1
  Pres.: Mr. Antonin Dvorak
  Dir.: Dr. Eva Soukupova
  Sec.: Ms. J. Gabrielova
  tel.: 619.68 & 611.75 & 639.68

Denmark
Danish Centre of the ITI
Ny Østergade 12-3
1101 Copenhagen K
  Pres.: Mr. Jens Louis Petersen
  Sec.: Ms. Bette Bjerregaard
  tel.: 12 48 48 (10-15h)
  (closed in July)

Egypt
Egyptian Centre of the ITI
Ezbekieh Theatre
Ataba
Cairo
  Pres.: Mr. Tewfik El Hakim
  Sec. Gen.: Mr. Nabil El Alfy

Finland
Finnish Centre of the ITI
Vuorikatu 6 A
Helsinki
  Pres.: Mr. Arvi Kivimaa
  Dir.: Ms. Riitta Seppälä
  tel.: 66 09 08 & 66 29 56
  cable: TEATTERI

France
French Centre of the ITI
7 rue du Helder
75009 Paris
  Pres.: Mr. Jean-Louis Barrault
  Sec. Gen.: Mr. Paul-Louis Mignon
  tel.: 770 39 84 (14.30-18.30h)

German Democratic Republic
GDR Centre of the ITI
Oberwallstr. 6/7
108 Berlin
  Pres.: Prof. Kayser
  Dir.: Mr. Walter Kohls
  Sec.: Mr. Wolf Eberman
  tel.: 207 13 74 (week: 9-17h)
  Cable: TEATRCENTR BERLIN

Germany, Federal Republic of
ITI Centre in the FRG
Bundesallee 23
1000 Berlin 31
  Pres.: Mr. Ivan Nagel
  Dir.: Mr. Joachim Werner Preuss
  tel.: 0311/86 03 48
  (Tuesday-Friday: 10-13h
  Monday: 15-18h)

Greece
Greek Centre of the ITI
P.O. Box 905
rue Chalkokondyli 36
Athens 102
  Pres.: Mr. Alcibiades Margaritis
  Sec. Gen.: Mr. Thanassis
  Papageorgiou
  tel.: 523 58 59 (week: 12-14h)

Hungary
Hungarian Centre of the ITI
c/o National Theatre
Hevesi Sandor ter.2
Budapest 1077
  Pres.: Mr. Endre Marton
  Sec.: Ms. Suzanne Gal
  tel.: 413849

Iceland
Icelandic Centre of the ITI
Leikfelag Reykjavikur
Reykjavik Theatre - Iono
Vonarstraeti 3
Reykjavik
  Pres.: Mr. Sveinn Einarsson
  Sec. Gen.: Ms. Vigdis
  Finnbogadottir
  Sec.: Mr. Klemenz Jonsson

India
Indian Centre of the ITI
Bharatiya Natya Sangh
F-34 Shanker Market
New Delhi 110001
  Pres.: Mr. Iqbal Mohammed Khan
  Sec. Gen.: Mr. Reoti Saran Sharma

Iran
Iranian Centre of the ITI
Faculty of Dramatic Arts
291 ave. Jalé-Abé-Sardar
Teheran
  Pres.: Mr. Mehdi Forough

Iraq
Iraqi Centre of the ITI
Iraqi Broadcasting Television and
  Cinema Establishment
Salhiyah
Bagdad
  Pres.: Mr. Youssif Al-Ani

Israel
Israeli Centre of the ITI
227 Dizengoff str.
Tel Aviv
  Pres.: Mr. Hanoch Bartov
  Dir.: Ms. Judith Gottlieb
  (Sunday-Thursday 8.30-12.30h)

Italy
Italian Centre of the ITI
1 Via della Consulta
Rome
  Pres.: Mr. Vincenzo Torraca
  tel.: 489 546 & 476 195

Japan
Japanese Centre of the ITI
c/o Nippon Engeki Kyokai
Kyoei Bldg.
Tsukiji 4-7-7 Chuo-Ku
Tokyo 104
  Pres.: Mr. S. Takahashi
  Vice-Pres.: Mr. Hideji Hojyo
  Sec. Gen.: Mr. T. Tobari
  tel.: 541 85 28

Jordan
Jordanian Centre of the ITI
Director Department of Culture &
  Arts
Ministry of Information
P.O. Box 6140
Amman
  Mr. Abdul-Rahim O'mer

Republic of Korea
Korean Centre of the ITI
P.O. Box 3828
Seoul
  Pres.: Mr. Suk-kee Yoh
  Vice-Pres.: Mr. Jeong-OkKim
  tel.: 25 9280

Monaco
ITI Centre in Monaco
C1Bis, Bd Albert 1er
Monaco
  M. Guy Brousse
  tel.: 30 18 80

Netherlands
Netherlands Centre of the ITI
Herengracht 166-168
Amsterdam
  Pres.: Mr. Donald R. Bleyleve
  Dir.: Mr. Max Wagener
  tel.: 23 51 04 (week: 9-17.30h)
  Cable: INTERTHEATER

Nigeria
Nigerian National Centre of the ITI
University of Ibadan
Dept. of Theatre Arts
Ibadan
  Mr. Joël Adedeji
  tel.: 62550, ext. 10.20
  Cable: UNIBADAN

Norway
Norwegian Centre of the ITI
  Radhusgaten 8
Oslo 1
  Pres.: Mr. Gerhard Knoop
  Dir.: Mr. Torbjørn Hersoug
  tel.: 02/42 28 68 (Monday-Friday
  10-14h)

Philippines
Philippine Centre of the ITI
Philippine Educational Theatre
  Association
Knights of Columbus Building
1000 Beaterio, Intramuros
Manila
  Sec.: Virgilio Catoy
  tel.: 494-637

Poland
Polish Centre of the ITI
Moliera 1
00-076 Warsaw
  Pres.: Mr. Janusz Warminski
  Sec. Gen.: Mr. Zygmunt Hübner
  tel.: 26 17 71 (week: 10-14h)

Rumania
Rumanian Centre of the ITI
9 rue Episcipiei
Bucarest 8000
  Pres.: M. Radu Beligan
  Sec.: Ms. Margareta Barbutza

Senegal
ITI Centre in Senegal
Theatre Sorano
B.P. 3243
Dakar
  Mr. Alioune Diop

Spain
Spanish Centre of the ITI
Tamayo y Baus 4
Madrid 4
  Pres.: M. Joaquin Calvo-Sotelo
  Sec. Gen.: Mr. S. Bautista de
  la Torre
  tel.: 419 47 46 (week: 11-13h)

Sweden
Swedish Centre of the ITI
Svensk Teaterunion
Birger Jarlsgatan 53
11145 Stockholm
  Pres.: Mr. Lars Af Malmborg
  Dir.: Ms. Ann Mari Engel
  tel.: 08/24 30 80

Switzerland
Swiss Centre of the ITI
Case Postale 193
1000 Lausanne 17
  Pres.: Ms. Lydia Benz-Burger
  Sec.: Mr. Charles Apothéloz
  tel.: 021 34 12 66

Syria
Syrian Centre of the ITI
Ministry of Culture
Damascus
  Pres.: Mr. Assa'ad Fedda

Turkey
Turkish Centre of the ITI
Unesco Bürosu
7/9 Goreme Sokak
Kavaklidere
Ankara
  Pres.: Mr. Mushin Ertugrul

U.S.A.
American Centre of the ITI
1860 Broadway, 15th floor
New York, N.Y. 10023
  Pres.: Ms. Rosamond Gilder
  Dir.: Ms. Martha Coigney
  Asst. Dir.: Ms. Peggy C. Hansen
  tel.: 245 3950 (week: 9.30-17.30)
  Cable: ROSGILD

U.S.S.R.
USSR Centre of the ITI
c/o VTO Gorki 16/2
Moscow K9
  Pres.: Mr. Mikhail Tsarev
  Sec.: Mr. Valery G. Khasanov
  tel.: 229 00 35 (week: 10-18h)
  Cable: USSR MOSCOW VTO

Venezuela
Venezuelan Centre of the ITI
Apartado 51-456
Caracas 105
  Pres.: Ms. Otero Silva
  Sec. Gen.: Mr. Herman Lejter

Yugoslavia
Yugoslav Centre of the ITI
c/o Republicke zajedrica kulture
Vase Miskina
71000 Sarajevo
  Pres.: Luka Pavolic
  Vice-Pres.: Mladja Vaselinovic
  Sec. Gen.: Asaf Dzanic
  tel.: (071) 39-760 or 38-892

Zaire
ITI Centre in Zaire
B.P. 8332
Kinshasa I
  Pres.: Mr. Viminde Segbia
  Sec. Gen.: Prof. Mobyem Mikanza

INDEX

This index serves both Volumes III and IV. Roman numerals indicate volume numbers; Arabic numerals refer to pages.

Fiske, Daniel W., III, 109
Fiske, Harrison G., III, 109
Fitz [pseudonym?], III, 109
Fitzgerald, Geraldine, III, 47, 50-2, 56-8
F. Jasmine Adams, III, 52
Flack, Binnie, III, 109
Flaherty International Film Seminar, III, 28
Flanagan, Hallie Ferguson, III, 5
Flears, Charles, III, 109
Fleck, Johann Friedrich Ferdinand, IV, 60
Fleischer, Richard, III, 86
Fleischman, Stanley, III, 66
Fleisser, Farieluise, IV, 65
Fletcher, John, III, 132
Flicker, Theodore J., III, 96
Flohr, W. Henry, III, 109
Florio, John, III, 136
Flower, C.E., III, 109, 128
Flynn, Errol, IV, 2
Folsey, George J., III, 66
Fonda, Henry, III, 48, 66
Fontane, Theodor, IV, 70
Foote, M., III, 109
Foote, Mary N., III, 109
Foote, Samuel, III, 140
Foote, William, III, 140
Forbes, Bryan, III, 66
Ford, Glenn, III, 66
Ford, John, III, 132-133
Ford, John T., III, 109
Ford, Nancy, III, 50
Forde, Florrie, IV, 3
Foreman, Carl, III, 66
Foreman, Jack, III, 66
Foreman, Richard, III, 54
Forrest, Edwin, III, 140
Fosse, Bob, III, 52
Foster, Annie, III, 109
Foster, Augusta, III, 109
Foster, L.F.S., III, 109
Fowler, Gene, III, 66
Fowler, Marjorie, III, 66
Fox, Henry J., III, 109
Fox, Stuart, IV, 22
Foxe, John, III, 136
Fragments of a Trilogy, The Trojan Women, III, 56
Fraker, William, III, 67
Frampton, Hollis, III, 25-6, 28-9, 31
Francis, M., III, 109
Francis, Saul W., III, 109
Frank [pseudonym?], III, 109
Frank, Leonard, IV, 66
Frankenheimer, John, III, 67
Franklin, Thomas, III, 133
Frankovich, Michael, III, 67
Franzoni, J.D., III, 109
Fraser, John, III, 141
Frazier, Mrs. J.W., III, 109

Fredericks, William S., III, 109
Frederickson, Gray, III, 67
Free and Accepted Masons, III, 105
Freed, Arthur, III, 67, 96
Freed, Bert, III, 67
Freeman, Y. Frank, III, 96
Freiberger, Fred, III, 87
French, Fanny, III, 109
French, Mrs. Mary L., III, 109
French, Wilfred A., III, 109
Freud, Sigmund, III, 37
Freytag, Gustav, IV, 70
Friedberger, Alfred, III, 109
Friedkin, William, III, 67
Friedlander, Erich, IV, 58
Friedman, Tully, III, 67
Frohman, Charles, III, 42-3, 48
Froissart, John, III, 136
Fronde, J.A., III, 109
Frost, David, IV, 2
Frothingham, O.B., III, 109
Froug, William, III, 67, 77
Frye, William P., III, 109
Fuentes, Carlos, III, 37
Fuhr, Lina, IV, 70
Fulkerson, A., III, 109
Fuller, George F., III, 109
Fuller, John, III, 109
Fuller, Sam, III, 67
Fulton, Henry K., III, 109
Furness, H.H., III, 104, 109, 129
Furness, Walter R., III, 130
Furnivall, F.J., III, 109, 129
Furth, George, III, 51

Gabrille [pseudonym?], III, 109
Gage, N.H., III, 109
Gage, W.L., III, 109
Game, Mateo, III, 109
Garber, Davis, III, 109
The Garden of the Finzi-Continis, IV, 21
Gardenia, Vincent, III, 52
Gardner, Herb, III, 67
Gardner, Robert, III, 25, 28, 30
Garfein, Jack, III, 67
Garnett, Tay, III, 87
Garrett, R.B., III, 109
Garrett, R.P., III, 109
Garrett, Thomas E., III, 140
Garrick Club. *See* Junior Garrick Club
Garrick, David, III, 140
Garrington, R.M., III, 109
Garson, Greer, III, 67
Gasparin, Catherine V., III, 138
Gates, Larry, III, 53
Gaudí, Antonio, IV, 9
Gauthier, Guy, III, 37
Gauthier, Xavière, III, 37
Gayler, Charles, III, 104
Gazul, Clara, III, 133
Geare, Randolph I., III, 109-110